THE MEANING OF GOLF

Craig Morrison

John Campion

Craig Morrison

The Meaning of Golf was first published as an ebook in 2017. It has been revised and updated in 2019 and made available by Forsythia Publishing as a paperback, audiobook and ebook.

themeaningofgolf.com

forsythia.co.uk

ISBN 9781092904612

United Kingdom 2019

To Andrew and Gene, who like golf books

Craig Morrison

CONTENTS / CARD OF THE COURSE

1 TOM, 3550

What is the meaning of golf?

It's a disappointment, rarely entirely gratifying. It always sees us hit imperfect shots and we believe we have let ourselves down. In all accounts of the greatest rounds, the sub-par rounds, the sub-60s even, there appears always to have been the possibility of at least one stroke less. The world's best golfer in 2000, when winning 12 tournaments, reckoned he hit only one perfect shot in an entire season.

So, golf is a game of mishits, but in this way it's a great pleasure, the perfect pursuit. It is exceedingly satisfying because it leaves us, ultimately, unsatisfied. And we crave more. It's crack cocaine (though some drug addicts function more effectively than golfers: burning less money, spending less time away from loved ones, being more effective in the workplace...)

In golf each shot is unique. In basketball, say, every

free throw is made from the same spot, the same distance in a similar environment. This cannot be said of golf where every strike is quite different. That much is obvious when one considers climatic conditions, laws of probability, the competitive circumstances, the endlessly different courses worldwide... In this way golf teaches us adaptability.

Golf worked for poor shepherds in Scotland just as it works for bankers spending their weekends in The Hamptons. It reminds all of us that whatever we want for will ultimately be deprived us. The first economic principle is that people always want more. It's part of the human condition. And golf – in spite of the luxury it sometimes affords us and the sums it can cost us – always bites back, reminding us we can't have everything. In this way it's spiritual. Through golf we can measure ourselves not wholly by money, not even by happiness. It sees us measure ourselves against nature, or an approximation of nature, and we find ourselves reassuringly wanting. Can we live with ourselves? Can we stand the truth of exactly what and who we are? Is it possible to know one's weaknesses, one's failings, and still carry on? This is the sort of stuff one might learn in a life and death situation. At a push we get some ideas about it in the middle of a long training run. But we can learn a little of such things through golf as well. When fully engaged with golf it begins to ask questions of us.

Golf is both trivial and significant. To be germane about it, golf is a game in which one tries to put a small ball into a hole from different distances, eighteen times, in as few shots as possible, the shots being struck with a variety of implements (varyingly unfit for the purpose is the usual addendum). To take a grander view, to look for the significance, golf is the most interesting of all sports, the one in which demanding physical skills – dexterity and timing especially – must be used alongside considerable mental skills, not exactly intellectual ability, but at least the ability to control or quieten the mind.

It cannot be sold to those who don't play it. The elevator pitch for the game, the one just proposed, is not great. But many exquisite joys are inexplicable to the uninitiated. Who really liked their first strong drink, their first cigarette? A favourite piece of music - one's desert island disc - is rarely a tune so catchy it was appreciated at first listening. The hit single (to use a dated term), doesn't always last like the trickier album track (to use another). Golf is like that. There are barriers to entry which, when overcome, increase its desirability. For the first-time player, unless their inaugural strike takes glorious flight, golf's appeal is not obvious. But it grows on you, like a dangerous illness. Hopefully, you learn to live with it.

Like all good pursuits it is impossible to master. Even golfing mediocrity is tough to achieve. Despite that, in fact because of it, golf is endlessly appealing to those who will embrace it. But it's not easy to love. Falling for golf is a bit like falling for your kidnapper. It's a kind of Stockholm Syndrome.

In strokeplay golf a round is constructed shot by shot. Like a house of cards, it doesn't take much for it to collapse. It begins hopefully with one passable strike out on to a suitably wide first fairway. The player then gingerly knocks one onto the first green. Two putts and they're on their way. They take the ignominy of some silly dropped shots and perhaps even make them up with a birdie or, depending on ambition, a smattering of pars. As the round goes on the importance of each shot grows. The validity of every shot already gone hangs on the one about to be played. Shot adds to shot until a bitter end or perhaps a sweet finale. But what's the use of 17 good holes and one shocker?

And so it is the player begins to 'feel the heat', to soak up pressure 'down the stretch'. After a run of great holes a golfer finds himself in uncharted waters and begins to panic... It might all be trivial in the grander scheme of things. Nobody dies. All concerned will get home to their beds just the same. But in the moment it is crushing. And in the moment, at the top of the game, a Major tournament perhaps, the heat is white hot, the sort of sensation few of us will ever know.

In cricket the batsman approaches a high score in a similar way, for a while at least, building his innings, each shot taking on increased importance. To get over the century is tough and when it happens it is monumental. But then the pressure's off. 110 runs is a glorious score. More would be better. But the anxiety is gone. Arguably the pressure's off when he has made what he knows to be an acceptable score. For the first few batters 50 might do. Tail-enders could be happy with 20. When they pass these scores they can relax. But in golf the burden only grows and the tension is there till the final putt drops.

In matchplay golf we can free ourselves of such fears. We play against our opponents, the overall tally not being part of the equation. Playing alone, we compete simply against ourselves and the course. But in all golfing formats we know, with complete clarity, if we've done well or otherwise. We don't need a scorecard or a result to tell us if we have done ourselves proud.

Golf is full of contradictions. Consider these. It is therapeutic but vexing. It can be cruel, torturing the mind, yet it is a pleasant escape. It might be played with friends but is in essence a solitary pursuit. And playing this sport well often leads to panic which in turn brings on poor play.

But golf's not a sport, is it? How can this inherently safe, low-impact, non-contact hobby be considered sport? You don't necessarily work hard, physically, when golfing. You don't really have to change your shoes. Surely, it's simply a pastime.

Yet golf's adherents believe it is a sport, a superior sport even (and not just in the attitudes of some of its snobbier institutions). Most definitions of sport refer to skill and physical exertion, competition in the name of entertainment. Older definitions relate to fun, as in 'he's a good sport.' Golf meets and exceeds the physical skills and competitive criteria while also functioning as a pastime for the less than athletic who happen to be good sports. That the battle between players is abstract, that it can be simply a player versus the course, that the winning is in numbers and not blows landed, puts off those want contact in their games. There's no actual physicality, no rough and tumble, yet most of us have met golf club secretaries we've wanted to punch. And many of us have thrown a club or at least an invective.

Anyway, let's call it a sport (not that it matters), a sport almost anyone can play because one doesn't have to break sweat or risk cardiovascular problems. And, as a result of its handicapping system, anyone, almost, can meaningfully play anyone else. In this way it's a good pursuit for those past their physical prime. Some say it's a game for old folks.

At the age of 59 Tom Watson was still breaking hearts. He was breaking the hearts of almost all who watched the 138th Open Championship at Turnberry in Scotland in 2009. His eight-foot putt to win on the 72nd slipped past the hole by less than an inch. A very nice man from Alabama won instead. But few were happy. The world wanted Tom Watson to win so that he might become, truly, The King of the Links, equalling Harry Vardon's six Open victories, not languishing tied in second place with Braid, Taylor and Thomson on a mere five apiece! The world wanted him to win so that we could relive one of the greatest champion-ships of all time, the 1977 event at the same course when he defeated Jack Nicklaus in a thrilling tête-à-tête. The world wanted him to win so that he would become the oldest winner of the tournament, put-ting Old Tom (the other one, Old Tom Morris of St Andrews) firmly into second place for his 1867 vic-tory age 46. It was meant to be a victory for age and wisdom and for the greatness of golf, a game in which those advanced in years can still compete, if not through strength then through grasp and guile. But it didn't happen. The winner sheepishly accepted his baubles. The crowd tried to smile. Only the runner-up himself seemed sanguine about it all. He had been in the moment. He hadn't waivered. He hadn't failed. A skip and jump from the golf ball as it landed on the final green had robbed him. Links golf is like that. Golf is like that. Life is like that.

Nine months earlier he had his left hip replaced. He had been in pain. Sleep wasn't easy. Walking wasn't easy. His golf swing was brittle. But post-surgery he almost became The Champion Golfer of 2009 (which is how they announce the winners of these things). He proved that great golf isn't the preserve of 21st century gym bunnies. And for years since that nearly-moment at Turnberry, he has been making the cut, posting some surprisingly low scores, frequently breaking his own record for oldest player to make the weekend at The Open.

For some, all this will be proof that golf isn't a sport.

For others it demonstrates golf's greatness, that it's a sport for a long life.

Golf doesn't stretch you, doesn't push or pull or batter you in any seriously damaging way, physically. No doubt many golfers have damaged knees, shoulders and hips through the ferocity of their swings and others have pulled a muscle picking up their bag. But the game doesn't exactly impact the player the way other games do. Boxers have their faces smashed up and their brains damaged. Rugby players break their necks. These can be wonderful, sometimes beautiful, sports. But the cost is high. A golfer's life is not usually compromised or shortened by the game.

Golf affords its followers a longevity many other sports simply don't. Many golfers, in old age, can still play similar shots to the ones they played in the flush of youth. At the outer limits of life our games will be diminished. Yet golf clubhouses aren't, generally, home to broken individuals reeling because their best days are behind them, guys who made the draft and then succumbed to injury, or high school heroes whose finest moments were in their teenage years. For these people – admittedly composites drawn from American movies! – competitive glory has been their thing and outside of golf that's something which is hard to recreate beyond a certain age.

Even as one's distance declines, one's strategic skills can improve. And as the shots add up the handicap grows so, even if it's manipulated, one can still stay in the hunt for various glories. In golf one can be super-annuated and streetwise. The grizzled old guy can still beat the young guy who hits it intercontinental.

At Turnberry, the runner-up's good grace told us that there's more to golf than winning, or at least that a gentleman might outwardly pretend as much. That's why for all his successes, for all the trophies on display back at the ranch in Kansas City, for all that he might tell his Ryder Cup teams behind closed doors, Tom was able to take this on the chin. It's not that he likes to lose. Early in his career, at the 1974 US Open, he held the 54-hole lead but failed at the final hurdle. At the same event the next year he equalled the competition's low scoring record at the halfway point but played the weekend 13 over. "Those consecutive US Opens made me hate losing. They taught me a lot and helped me figure out how to win," he says. Tom went on to clinch his first Major in that summer of '75, the Open Championship at Carnoustie.

He used to cry when he played badly or when he lost. But the boy became a man and he learned to lose without shedding tears and he learned to win without viciousness. He had to lose first in order to win later. That's how he came to be so good at closing out those big events. Others may have achieved full-on Major success earlier. But few have then built on them. Tom went on to collect eight career Majors. That's a US Open on the California coast. That's slipping into a green jacket twice. And it's those five Open Championships, four of them in Scotland. He's also won six Majors on The Champions Tour (pro golf for those of a certain age) including The Senior British Open on three occasions, each on a Scottish course. (Those shouldn't be forgotten. The average driving distance between the top-flight tours and their fifty-something counterparts is approximately 10 yards and the scoring difference is typically less than one shot per round. So beyond marketing dollars and television air time there's not much in it.)

Early in his career Tom acquired the nickname Huckleberry Dillinger, the joke being that the sweet, smiling, seemingly innocent exterior was so different from his interior steely resolve. It turns out that this is the best way to play the game: to be at once gentle but to get it done. The snarling and machismo on show in other sports – required in some other sports – doesn't work in golf. There's something to enjoy in the (sometimes staged) angry weigh-ins before boxing matches, but for many of us, golf's more interesting than that.

So a kid from Missouri becomes a grand old man of the game. He fought his battles inside himself, learned to come out on top and his great moments will live as long as the game itself. But ask Tom about his favourite memories and it's not just those monumental Majors which he remembers most fondly. Ask questions about the historical milestones and fairly soon he's back enthusing about some experiences which are comparatively incidental.

Golf's been a journey that's taken him from State Champion age just 17 to The Butler Cabin at Augusta National and the 18th green prize giving ceremony at Pebble Beach. But he's able to remember just as fondly the games as a boy with his father and his father's friends: "I've always enjoyed being around older people. They've got so much to offer. It's just that they're getting harder for me to find now."

Inevitably he thinks often of his long-time caddie and friend Bruce Edwards who died in 2004: "He was straight-talking with me, kept me on the straight and narrow in golf and in life even! We always laughed together. He was a brother to me."

There have been treks to western Ireland where his name will forever be associated with his beloved Ballybunion: "Every course architect needs to play there. It's like golf began there. And it's a true test."

He travelled there with his old mentor Byron Nelson and they went on to enjoy a memorable game at Rosses Point: "Both Byron and I loved County Sligo. The 14th hole is one of the great par-4s. We talked so much on that trip. I always learned from Byron. He told me that when you get nervous on the course you've got to slow right down. Walk slowly. Talk slowly. Do things deliberately and you'll soon settle down. That advice helped me in a lot of tense situations."

He's golfed in South West England with a close childhood friend who became general manager at St Eno-doc Golf Club. They went to play the ancient links at Westward Ho! too: "Many Americans make for Scotland and Ireland, but I've had some of my happiest times on those old courses in England with Tuck, taking it all in and reminiscing about days gone by."

And some journeys to Dornoch in the Scottish Highlands feature highly too: "I'd already won three Open Championships when I made it there the first time, so I knew links golf, but there's always so much more to learn. It was at the end of a glorious tour with my friend Sandy Tatum, a past President of the USGA, a wise golfer, and a real gentleman. We visited some favourite courses in Ireland and then came to Scotland where we finished up at Dornoch. It was preparation for the 1981 tournament in Kent. I wasn't playing especially well. I wouldn't go on to win at Sandwich. But I definitely developed a new appreciation for the links game."

Maybe his preparation for that tournament should have been a jot gentler. At Dornoch he signed countless autographs and staged an impromptu putting contest with the junior members. And he played three rounds in just 24 hours, reckoning it the most fun he'd had on a golf course. He had arrived planning just one game, but the allure of the course is considerable. Tom enjoys creative games. He was on the table tennis team at Stanford. And Dornoch is a course which encourages creativity, teaches it even.

So through golf Tom's travelled far and wide, in the spotlight and under the radar. He's won and he's lost though overall, by any standards, he's a true champion.

All golfers must lose more than they win. Tiger Woods, during periods at the top of the game, could win about 25% of the time. But the majority get nowhere near that. Tournament golf is the strangest thing. You mostly lose. Most players mostly lose. Most players never ever win.

But losing is in the nature of things. This isn't a fashionable statement. We're led to believe we can all be winners. But golf says, it's not like that. Gatsby doesn't get his girl and Hamlet's revenge is a trade-off. We fail and we compromise but there are successes on the road. To play golf is to know failure. To persevere with it is to know failures and successes and to learn from it is 'to treat those bedfellows just the same'.

For the majority of us the meaning of golf can't solely be in the winning. Maybe it's about taking part, learning some lessons, taking the rough with the smooth and other clichés. Maybe that's why the notion of stopping to smell the flowers on the way - as Walter Hagen or perhaps Ben Hogan suggested - has so effortlessly entered common usage. And maybe that's why their old adage is now mostly applied, not just to golf, but to life.

Golf is a struggle but also a great romance. It is a

game of endless promise. Each shot promises much. And even if the promise is broken, if the shot doesn't achieve what the player hoped for, there is a next time and a next... It might be an illusion. It's probably a form of self-delusion. But it feels real enough and it keeps even the most hopeless players coming back. Very few people - despite various threats - ever successfully, decisively, for all time, retire their clubs to the attic or an online auction.

If you're a tour player and your golf is off the mark it probably makes the sport unlovable: you have bills to pay, a family to feed (a private jet to fuel). But when playing for fun the misery is marginal, the negatives rarely outweighing the positives. Something good will happen soon, we feel. Inside all average golfers there's a great golfer waiting to get out.

It's important to have fun. It's important that we set aside time to play. In play, there's joy to be had. Through play, there are lessons to be learned. This isn't news. It's ancient philosophy. The Roman poet Ovid knew it. 'In our play we reveal what kind of people we are,' he wrote. The Greek philosopher Plato recognised it too. 'Life must be lived as play,' he said.

2 HIGH TIME, 3950

Here in Dornoch the chill mineral air is pure, beautiful to breathe, restorative to the body. And the championship course at Royal Dornoch Golf Club is thrilling to play, a tonic for the soul. Why is it special? Looking out to sea here, the Highlands and their mountains behind, most of the country below, only the wild remotest places north and beyond, you feel you are somewhere singular. If you're here, you've made an effort to get here and that alone makes it important. To enjoy something, you need to earn it, or at least that's what our parents told us. You've travelled from London or Glasgow or Edinburgh or somesuch to Inverness, the capital of the Highlands, and it's been a fair old journey. But then you've carried on, 45 miles north, over firths and bridges, past distilleries and fields of barley swaying in the breeze. You've crossed beyond the 57th parallel north. Maybe you've travelled from the other side of the world, spent many hours on an aeroplane? This place's reputation is such that international voices fill the air. It's high on the wish list for global golf connoisseurs.

The course more than lives up to its sterling reputation and enviable location. It has glorious rhythm, pleasing balance and entirely convincing sequence. There's an out and back linearity to it, yet there are clever discrepancies. It contains an interesting thread, like a really good book. But it has qualities that can only really be understood by playing it, the more times the merrier to fully appreciate it.

Trying to pinpoint a course's greatness is tricky. It's reminiscent of the once brilliant aphorism that writing about music is like dancing about architecture. I write about 'pleasing balance' and 'convincing sequence' and I know what I mean to say but many will be left wondering. It might be better to simply say this: Dornoch is a course which may shake your very being. If you can get here then it's high time you did.

It is a links course, so plays as the game was mostly enjoyed in earlier times, on the firm land close to the seashore. This sort of golf is almost always a joy, though there's much snobbery about it, a lot of nonsense spoken and written. Links golf is not the be all and end all, but it is special; it is rare; and it is a treat. A bit like single malt whisky, which is made only with barley - whereas grain whisky is made with almost any cereal - links golf is found only close to sandy coastland and is perhaps the finest form of the game. It's not the only thing, not the lone valid golf experience. But you should give it a go, ideally as soon as possible, before the ice shelves fall into the sea and these classic courses are drowned by rising seas. That said, there are only something like 250 links courses out of roughly 30,000 courses globally. So, most golfers never play the links game. Unfortunately, that majority are missing a small something. It's thrilling to be amongst the dunes: we do like to be beside the sea. And yet the dunes don't stand high here at Dornoch. The North Sea and the Dornoch Firth are visible from everywhere on the course because there's no mighty primary dune structure between the players and the waves. Rather, the elevation changes for which the course is famous are between those holes on high heathery plateaus and those found closer to sea-level. Marine terraces of various heights, covered in blown sand and natural grasses, make up the lie of the land. The firm fairways are, in parts, bordered by gorse bushes, bright yellow and fragrant through spring and summer, their delicious vanilla and coconut perfume sometimes surprising visitors. Dornoch's geology is glorious; the flora is fabulous; and its golfing proportions are perfect. The game's been played here for at least 400 years and the club was formally founded in 1887. But the dates don't matter. To be here is to know that the course has almost always been here, dreaming down the centuries.

Alan Grant, a local one-man university and ideas factory, says Royal Dornoch is a 1961 Château Margaux.

He may or may not have tasted the great Bordeaux, but there's some poetry and surely some truth to what he says. "It's elegant and it's precious. It stands the test of time. Comparisons are invidious but they're also inevitable. OK, so I could have chosen another wine. But it sounds good, don't you think?"

Alan defies classification, which is an excellent thing. But let me try to put you in the picture. He is strong and wiry, charmingly unkempt with a full mop of grey corkscrew curls, a moustache and, sometimes, the beatnik's soul patch between the chin and mouth! At any rate, he typically sports some facial hair and he has a glimmer in his eye. He's quick with a joke and deadly with a sand wedge.

He wasn't yet a golfer in 1981 when Tom Watson made that first visit and put his hometown on the map. In Dornoch that made him a little unusual, preferring fashion and football to the 18-hole game. However, his golfing interest developed when he returned to these parts following his Masters at The Royal College of Art in London and in 1984, at the ripe age of 30, Alan began to pick up the game, developing a stylish swing, delightfully floating yet deceptively powerful. Its output seems so much more than its input, which is a glorious thing in golf. His long fades fly far further than the languid action suggests. There is such a thing as the Dornoch Draw, the player setting up with the right foot back, hitting the controlled hook which stays low and runs out on the ground. But Alan draws a different arc in the skies. Without trying, he just seems to adopt an alternative approach.

This eighth-generation Dornoch man is from a long line of philosophising and farming clergymen, artists and golfers. If you're lucky enough to get a game with him and get to know him he begins to share his ideas. It makes you feel creative and hopeful, convincing you that golf is a game for inventive people. Like Dornoch itself, he has an energy about him.

The first hole on the course is that perfect thing, a short and simple par-4. And yet, because it's Royal Dornoch, because it's the first hole, I feel a little self-conscious in its presence. Self-consciousness ruins many efforts. Don't look down. Don't look into the faces of the audience. Dance like nobody's watching. Despite such worries I somehow hit one of my better shots, down within bump and run distance from the green and Alan offers congratulations. "You're well down there in a world of your own and that's a good place to be."

The second, a mid-range par-3, is one of golf's finest holes. Its green is of the upturned saucer-variety for which Dornoch is famous, except it's more like an upturned bowl, its sides sloping incredibly steeply away. Miss the green and you'll roll off down these slopes finishing far below the putting surface, the tall flag perhaps not even visible to you. Sometimes the side slopes are shaved tight so you might putt up them or fire a pitch into them. Sometimes they're grown out so the lob shot is required. Somehow I hit and hold the green from the tee and Alan offers commiserations. "It's a shame to come all this way and miss out on the hardest second shot in the game."

We walk to the third tee and the great moment arrives when the view fully opens up, the links displayed, the world at your feet. The horizon is huge and you feel that you can see the curve of the earth, the glories of our planet revealed. "This is where we show you true splendour and riches: all this can be yours that panorama promises. But fall not into temptation. Do not believe you can have this course your own way," he offers up.

The still point of the turning world seems sometimes to be the inside of the head at the top of the backswing, a peaceful place in the moment of transition when one is playing well and confidently and has achieved some central stillness. That's what I'm thinking stood on the third tee under endless skies. The drive on this long par-4 is inviting and asks for a running draw, my favourite shot. Despite the perfection of the time and the place, my imperfect golf intervenes and I wobble my head around while I swing and execute something quite different to the stroke imagined, a strange drive, a thin, low slice. I groan and complain that it's not as I'd planned. But wait, it trundles on and misses the bunkers and finds some short grass and, against the odds, it's in decent shape. "We shouldn't really speak before the ball stops moving," Alan suggests, smiling somewhat sagely. Silence is sometimes seemly. The almost topped shot was shameful but it turned out well enough. Silence returns us to dignity: one of golf's many little learnings.

The fourth is best played with a draw too and again my ineptness intrudes. By the time I get to the putting surface I've played a few shots too many. It's an interesting green and it teaches you that there are many ways to hole a putt: up and over a hill slowly or maybe faster along the bottom of a slope. There are smaller subtleties too, the difference between true north and magnetic north, a whisker one way or the other. Despite some good guidance I make quite a sizeable score. "The first six holes at Dornoch speak to one another," Alan says. "After the first two you should really have been expecting these dropped shots. It's the way of things here. One hole might give something, but others will take it back."

This sort of chat, elsewhere, from someone else, might raise a few eyebrows. But here, from Alan, it's pretty convincing. It's funny though because some years ago, when the curator of an art exhibition told me his paintings have dialogue with one another, I felt a bit nauseous.

From the elevated tee on the fifth hole, the fairway below looks so perfectly bunkered that I hold my breath for a moment when I set eyes on it. Anyone would want to hit a lovely shot here and, happily, I do. The ball is in the air, on the wing, ludicrously high, slapped, to its surprise, high into the sky, and time stands still before it eventually, finally, falls vertically, landing short of the bunkers. I adored that shot! For a moment time was not bearing us away. The white dot soared and stopped for a second in the sky.

I wonder how far I've got to the green. I don't use my phone or my watch or pull out a rangefinder or call out to Alan "hey, what's the number?" But I do reach into my bag for my 'strokesaver,' the now rather quaint printed course planner with yardages and contours. I wave the book at Alan. "The book of truth!" he exclaims. He's been playing this course forever. He has natural advantages. But also, he believes well the dictum that 'the map is not the territory.' Numbers would only interfere with that natural flow of things which he prefers. He's interested in science, but his approach is firstly artistic.

"Whinny Brae is where the overture of the early holes concludes," says Alan, surveying the splendid sixth hole, a single-shotter to a green perched on a ledge with ferns and whins covering the hillside above it to the left and a long fall-off to the right. There's not a lot to hit and almost nowhere to miss. "The par-3s here, the four ladies of Dornoch, are the key to scoring well," he says, with meaning.

Alan thinks golf clubs should have names and not numbers. He's not talking about the tradition of named clubs which died out in the 20s, the niblick and the mashie and the gentleman's persuader. Rather, he's thinking of each golfer being able to name his own clubs, stamping unique and personal titles on them, nomenclature instead of numerals printed on the side or the sole. "It's another way to express yourself, a bit of fun. And over time you'd relate better to each club's purpose. Without the numbers you're into the realms of something different. It's the same with specific yardages. Learn to live without them and you flow more easily!

"There are just too many numbers in golf," he continues. "I actually looked into doing this, in a business sense, sketching out some plans with a golf manufacturer. But it came to nothing. The single run doesn't work. You can get blank ones mind you and engrave them..."

Alan suggests some names, all comedic, all slightly obscene. I suggest some with a literary angle – Rogue Male and Clockwork Orange - but Alan worries that I might be scorned by caddies, not realising that I'm already scorned by caddies.

When not dreaming up great wheezes, Alan has a day job, a day job which is also a night job at Skibo Castle, the home of The Carnegie Club, a private and pricey Dornoch retreat for the jet-set. It's there, to some 400 lucky and very wealthy souls, that he is front-of-house guy, the host with the most, intellectual and comic, a very 21st century court clown. The motley patterned outfit and the three-pointed jingle-belled cloth cap are missing, yet he has always made his own distinctive clothes. He doesn't carry the mock sceptre ('the bauble') of earlier royal jesters, but he often golfs on the Carnegie Links with just two or three clubs under his arm, walking the course and joining up with his international guests for just a few holes, no doubt perfectly striking the balance between charm and cheek, comedy and pathos, informing and entertaining about Scotland's gift of golf to the world as well as his beloved Royal Dornoch.

Like Shakespeare's Fest, the clown of Twelfth Night, Grant is 'wise enough to play the fool', which allows him to mock the most prominent without penalty. Many members at Skibo, ironically, pay their money to be treated normally, and Alan does just that. Yet out of these professional relationships great friendships have grown up.

"It's a mistake to think rich people are more interesting than us ordinary folk," he cautions. "But the ones with their own golf courses and vineyards are admittedly fun to be around!"

It was Andrew Carnegie, then the world's richest man, who built Skibo Castle as we know it now, all fairytale turrets and classical pillars. It was here, at the end of the 19th Century, and rather late in his life, that he got the golf bug, got it bad. Dornoch can have that effect on people and Carnegie came to believe that golf was 'a necessary adjunct of civilisation.' That might seem to be overstepping the mark. Greek and Roman cultures managed ok without it. But for sure he was onto something. Golf is civilised and civilising. It offers a wide spectrum of pleasure, interest, education, personal accountability and self-improvement perhaps. And Carnegie was all about individual improvement, donating colossal sums of money to build thousands of libraries globally.

I've inflicted my unpredictable golf game onto the championship links at Dornoch on a few occasions now. Mostly I've done no lasting damage to the course. Occasionally, I've even got the better of the course, for a couple of holes. What has never happened though, and surely never will happen, is that I've tired of it. Another thing that's never happened: I've never parred the 14th hole, Foxy. Golf's a tricky and enigmatic game and this is a tricky and enigmatic hole: Foxy by name and foxy by nature. It never ceases to amaze me (and whenever I play it my golf constantly ceases to amaze me). "You hit two decent shots there," Alan reckons, kindly, pityingly. "The tempo was great, but the magic which Foxy requires just didn't materialise."

In golf we need rhythm and we need timing and these cannot be taught. Playing golf at Dornoch the golfer is exposed to a course which is rhythmical and perfectly timed in terms of its challenges. The atmosphere is relaxed and one's golf, perhaps, takes on some of these qualities. Alan, for example, swings with considerable grace. The talk is often about golf swings, though rarely the technicalities, often just the manner and the groove. The golf swing, in a golf town like Dornoch, is to be watched and considered.

Historic swings are discussed. Changes in the swing are spoken about. But there's not so much talk here about swing speed and ball speed, not a lot of jargon. The louche style of Freddie Couples is mentioned. "He golfs like a black woman dancing," Alan says. There's no racism or sexism in Alan Grant and he doesn't go in for stereotyping either. But he likes to say interesting things.

Our 18 holes are nearing completion. "You've not lived, really, until you've walked down the last hole at Dornoch in the gloaming," he offers. "Probably no sensory experience matches up to, let's say, sex, certainly the first time, or maybe, better still, being born, or one's dying seconds. But amongst the less apocalyptic pleasures a birdie under a full moon on the 18th green at Royal Dornoch would certainly set the nerve endings tingling."

It's only lunchtime in April. But someday I hope to lash a 3-iron into the gathering darkness at midnight in midsummer and find my ball lying close to the hole.

A game with Alan is always great, as much an art event or happening as it is a round of golf! In the car park a look inside the trunk of his 1980s Porsche reveals an accidental art installation: vintage clothes, a guitar and those rubber shoes worn by doctors with the words 'If Found Please Return to The Fox Club' written on them. I have no idea.

We sign off for now and I'm already looking forward

to doing it again. I think of how Alan signs off his emails. Alan The Grant. IMAGRANT etc. Always interesting. Like the place itself.

The people of Dornoch, to perhaps generalise, are less taciturn and tricky than in many remote Scottish spots. All are welcome here. It's not just a great course but a great club too. It's not been overrun by pushy people and despite its fame it's still a friendly local hangout. Sometimes, out golfing on a great course, one is then struck, when coming back into the clubhouse, at how strange these places can be, that on the course, within certain guidelines naturally, one is free, alive, and then in the clubhouse there's a stiffness, a hierarchy which irritates. But that's not the case here. Dornoch is, first and foremost, a member's club. Its members are ordinary local folk who play fast, play well and can cope with a wee breeze. Its members also include international types, a large overseas members section made up of well-to-do golf fanatics from around the world who come here because it's good for them to keep it real now and again.

That said, you don't want to get on the wrong side of the members. I well remember the black looks I got on the first tee when – by special dispensation – a new Chinese friend and I squeezed our way out onto the course with a non-existent tee time just in front of a member's foursomes morning. The glowers were because Ling, the editor of China's biggest golf magazine, took a few air shots before trundling a ball pathetically down the fairway. He had the look of a man who didn't play much golf and, indeed, that turned out to be the case. He took a lot of shots. He took a lot of photographs too. But playing 'better-ball' off the tee and walking fast we kept ahead of the members and all was well. Ling reckoned he'd never been anywhere so lovely. I'm pretty sure he'd never played a round so fast either.

Back in China Ling's parent were 'workers' and I learned that golf is not a massive deal in his country, not growing as fast as western golf industry entrepreneurs hope. And the obstacle is money. He reckons the average annual salary is £2,000 and the average green fee £100. He believes most of the country's golfers have only ever played on a driving range. Ling himself could use a bit more range time, but he's been busy learning about the game. He's outrageously knowledgeable, great company too. He knows everything about the architecture of Britain's historic golf sites, mostly courses he's never played and can hardly pronounce. He knows a lot about the contemporary professional game too. His enthusiasm for it all is massive, yet the opportunities for golf in China simply don't abound, even in his job!

Our round complete, I ask Ling for the car keys, the hire car keys I'd handed him before we teed off when he needed to change quickly from his tracksuit trousers. He's lost them. I rushed him. He's sorry. I'm sorry. The rental car company is sorry and unforgiving. I have a train to catch back in Inverness. Ling has a flight to catch. It's a very expensive disaster for sure.

But in the clubhouse my boyhood friend, Andrew Skinner, the head professional, whose father Willie was head professional for decades before him, sets to work. Neil, the club manager, is called in to help with the search. Members are rallied. The clock ticks down and minutes from the outer limits of the last possible departure time, the keys are found, dropped behind a pair of shoes in the locker room.

Things always come good in Dornoch. There's something good, something great even, about the place.

Heading south towards Inverness, the Highland capital, praying not to get stuck behind a tractor, Ling talks me through the history of golf-like games in China where not dissimilar pastimes have long existed. There are pictorial and written records from more than 1,000 years ago when something called Chuiwan was played, a very involved form of putting rather than one concerned with distances. Ling says an improbable theory exists that Mongolian travellers may have brought this game to Scotland, a game with balls, with holes and with a selection of sticks. Its case as the antecedent for modern golf is therefore compelling. Ling doesn't buy it. But he thinks that if the Chinese government were to be persuaded of it they'd be less inclined to crack down on the game, intermittently criminalising it or banning their employees from playing it. Mission Hills, China's largest golf facility, the world's largest golf facility, is a major financial backer of the Special Collections at The University of St Andrews, specifically its significant golf archive. Perhaps the game's history will one day be newly understood and China will have no small part to play in it. Perhaps 'the green opium' once feared by the Communist regime will be allowed to thrive in China.

But however it's written and whoever writes it, golf's history will always include this northerly outpost. Dornoch's place in golf's grand scheme is secure. Out on the edge, but central to the game, it forever resonates with all who visit.

3 EMPLOYED, 3370

It's January and I've escaped Northern Europe. I'm in Florida for work purposes and I've got time to kill before that work kicks in: a golfer's dream situation, really.

Three days before my meetings begin I've checked into an Orlando motel. There'd been hopes of a game at Seminole as a guest of a friend of a friend, but, force majeure, it's not going to happen. It would have been fun to head down the coast towards Juno Beach, to feel the ocean breezes. And it would have been exciting to play that famous course, to meet some of the lucky members and see the glorious clubhouse. But some good will come of these changed plans and I can now relax in Orlando for a couple more days and I'm going to find somewhere else to play, somewhere less swanky so I can be spared the awkward shame of having people carry my clubs and polish my shoes.

I'd been counting on Seminole for a couple of reasons. It would be an item ticked off the greedy or ambitious golfer's bucket-list: a great day's golf and a lifetime's golfing bombast. Also, it was my chance to go and play one of Donald Ross's most celebrated courses.

In 1899, when golf in America was just a decade old, Donald Ross made the trip across the Atlantic, taking his expertise to foreign shores because he'd been advised by a regular visitor to Scotland, a Harvard Professor, that he could bring in $60 a month there, plus 50 cents an hour for lessons, much more than he could earn back home. Ross had reckoned on developing and running a course in Massachusetts, The Oakley Country Club, which he did for a short time. But a year later he was developing Pinehurst where he would be resident professional. He would become one of America's greatest course architects, designing almost 400 of them before he died in 1948.

Born in Dornoch, born to golf, Ross had been a trainee carpenter before going to St Andrews where he worked for Old Tom Morris who taught him club-making and greenkeeping. Before emigrating to America he'd returned to Dornoch where he became 'keeper of the green'.

Donald Ross, who did so much to popularise the game in the US, is the link between Old Tom Morris, the father of the game, and Jack Nicklaus, the greatest champion in the game, because it was Ross, Old Tom's apprentice remember, who designed Scioto, young

Jack's place of learning. Anyway, Donald Ross and his courses are of no small importance and I'm anxious to play one. There are plenty to choose from because only Massachusets and North Carolina have more of his designs than Florida. Sure, I'm here to work, but playing a Donald Ross course is work, kind of, because I'll be writing about it. And I could use the winter sunshine, the vitamin D temporarily unavailable in the British Isles.

The course I settle on, after the most cursory online research, is up in Sanford, not so far from the I-4. Others seem far grander, but this one is open to visitors, inexpensive and, crucially, mostly unchanged since it was built in 1922, which makes it one of Florida's older courses. It's been a little improved through the years, but not fatally altered, not least because, enclosed by roads and housing, the space isn't available. So it's short, though it hosted PGA tournaments back in the day, before clubmaking was taken out of the hands of Donald Ross and his peers and into the hands of scientists. Hagen, Sarazen, Hogan, Palmer and other greats have played here. Add my name to that list, I think, as I drive north, closing the car windows to cross the road bridge over Lake Jesup which is swarming with insects.

Mayfair Country Club turns out to be, culturally, somewhere between a driving range on the Panhandle and Pinehurst itself. It's a country club, but low-key and friendly. I play with two locals, a labourer who's already finished work for the day and a tennis pro who has no bookings. They're great guys, great golfers. The course is wide open. Hurricanes took out hundreds of trees at the turn of the century, they tell me. We all play well. We all have fun. No money changes hands but there are a couple of beers in the clubhouse afterwards. Like the song, it's a place where everybody knows your name. "Craig, where's that accent of yours from?" someone asks me. "He's not from round here," one of my playing partners explains. "OK, must be from Daytona," the guy at the bar reassures everyone. It's a great golf experience, agreeable and authentic. Except it turns out not to be so authentic...

"No, this isn't a Donald Ross course," the tennis pro tells me. Others make counterclaims. But he says it's not, that there's been an historical mix up. "This place used to be The Seminole Country Club. Somewhere, somehow, someone got confused. This isn't Seminole." Turns out the golf club has been trading on a fiction and there's even been a lawsuit concerning it. The Donald Ross name means a management company can charge higher green fees. Without it the prices go down. The city of Sanford had been selling an error. Makes sense: I travelled to play a Donald Ross design. Yet it also makes no sense: I couldn't be happier with what I found here. "It was some Scottish guy who designed it though, Cuthbert Butchart they think. Doesn't matter, does it? These guys were designing courses all over the place on the back of coasters," he says, replacing his drink on one. And he's right. It doesn't matter. Every course is different and if you're one of the good guys, someone who simply enjoys some golf, then you'll often find the best in every course. I loved Mayfair Country Club. It couldn't have been better if Donald Ross himself had shown me round the place. Do the greens slope back to front like the first at Dornoch? Are they domes, upturned saucers like the second at Dornoch? No. But you know what? It's charming and good fun. It's not high-end. But who wants high-end all the time? It's a good thing, sometimes, to dance with the girls who aren't being danced with.

An interest in a course architect is not some type of pretension. Architects are artists, their work – over many years and membership subscriptions and visitor green fees – taking on the value of a Rubens or Rembrandt. Their styles, at their best, can be distinctive, instantly recognisable: in Ross's case, those back-to-front sloping greens and upturned saucers. There's a value in it which has been recognised since Old Tom Morris, golf's first real celebrity, put his name to course designs. But I'm not certain its commercial value was fully appreciated before Robert Trent Jones advertised his services in a golf trade magazine with the line 'get yourself an RTJ Signature Course.' Donald Ross wasn't paid a fortune for his work, though it's worth a fortune now. But sometimes the work of the unknown artist, the committees down the years, the small changes made by greenkeepers, are just as valid as the solo work of a big-name designer. It might still be a great wine, just not a single vineyard or single grape variety. Consider this too: many great poetry treasuries start with those gems written by 'anonymous'.

Next day – still days to kill - I drive to Bay Hill to take a look around. Like all visitors, I'm hoping to spot Arnold Palmer, but I hear he's unwell and seen less and less. Later in the year the great man will be dead. His work took him all over the world, but Bay Hill is the centre of Arnold Palmer Enterprises, the most successful golf business ever created by a golfer, with course design at its core. A signature Palmer design is a course worth having, but we all know his expert partners worked alongside him.

I hit balls on the range. I'm not a great range guy, but I get into the rhythm and set myself tasks, 50 yard bump and runs, 60 yard lobs, fades, draws, all executed poorly, but each one approached carefully, with as much concentration as I can muster. In this way the minutes fly by like a golf ball lashed far down the fairway by Palmer in his prime. This kind of endeavour is a form of joyful if not gainful employment. The more I hit the better they get. Maybe the path to quality is quantity and I've wasted a winter without a single shot being struck. Soon though the quality tails off and I remember myself to be more of a word-order guy than the word-count type.

Palmer once said something about what people find in poetry and art and how he finds it in the flight of a good drive. I know what he means (though I'm quite at home with the occasional sonnet). In the afternoon I'm working on a different pitch, practising a speech, readying myself for the most important of my meetings. Time goes slow in my little room. Then I get to writing and time speeds up. Being creative, assembling something - be it a short story or a round of golf – gives enough substance to an activity to make it worthwhile. People in real jobs in actual cubicles would laugh at the notion that this is work, and the next day I'm labouring on golf courses again, playing from the back tees all day. That's not a way of saying something more meaningful, something about how I'd been up against it, something about the unfairness of life. I'm simply talking about 36 holes of golf played at their maximum length.

It wasn't vanity, though it may have been stupidity. Here, you see, was a rare chance to play two rounds of golf in one day on great courses in full sun, a chance to really see what a couple of championship challenges might look like from the tips. When I was out there, realising the size of the task, I should probably have switched to forward tees. It wasn't a competition; I wasn't exactly keeping score. But for reasons of stubbornness or superstition I chose not to. (I don't like changing tees during a round and if I start out on the tiger tees or championship tees then I almost always finish on them, albeit battered and bruised and swearing not to be so silly again.)

Making my way to the Hammock Beach courses up on

the Palm Coast I was excited at the prospect of it all. I was to be first off on the Ocean Course, the design of one Jack Nicklaus. Then there'd be time for a snack before a game on the Conservatory Course, the design of Jack's old friend and rival, one Tom Watson. Listening to local radio which, to my British sensibilities always sounds like something from another world (The Hog FM – classic rock), I was getting ready to hit some decent drives, maybe make a few birdies. The music (of a certain vintage and volume) was waking me up. Why would I not want to play every yard of Nicklaus and Watson golf course that would be available to me? And with Van Halen ringing in my ears, 600 yard golf holes would be no more than a drive (or two) and a wedge (or three or four).

Much more, I think, should be made of the journey to a golf course. It's a key component in the overall experience. That it's better to travel than to arrive may only occasionally be true, but it's frequently accurate to say that the build-up to a game of golf, the expectation of the shots to be executed, the anticipation and promise is often better than the reality.

Through the dawn, shaken awake by golf's most celebrated musical artists, (Aerosmith...), excitement was building nicely. Sure, this was travel to a family-friendly holiday resort and not some far flung romantic Irish links or New Jersey private place of privilege. But the little toll bridge over the Intracoastal Waterway is a nice touch. I was going somewhere special to play courses created by the greatest of the greats...

And it would be Florida golf of a surprisingly rare sort considering that it's the state with the longest coastline and the most golf courses. It would be seaside golf.

Following the formalities, I made my way to the first and some women approach me, native New Yorkers here for the winter, astonishingly well-preserved at maybe twice my age, 80 let's say. Apparently they've observed that I'm an international visitor. How? Well, I'm wearing shorts and it must be only 80 degrees. Honestly, I had no idea I stood out as such a tourist. I'm a cool customer I think and I'm wearing a pullover. But that doesn't cut it with the golden girls who are all in phenomenally expensive wind-proof jackets, wrapped up against the chill which I take for a heatwave.

The Ocean Course is excellent. The Bear Claw, its final four holes, gets all the plaudits, but for me the 9th is the hole I'd wrap up and take home. It plays parallel to the beach, which is where I hit my drive. I take a deep breath, reload and it's déjà vu (all over again, as Yogi Berra said). Still, it's a wonderful hole.

In the afternoon I make my way to the Conservatory Course. It's very manicured, manmade and downright mean. I've never been in so many bunkers. I've never been in so many perfect bunkers.

It's been instructive to learn what Nicklaus and Watson consider a course to be. The Nicklaus design is less brutal than the Watson. He's a tough cowboy, Tom. Playing their courses I've measured myself against these greats and found myself far short of greatness, sometimes short of the main hazards, occasionally short of breath. I should have played from the forward tees...

It's January and at this time of year the golf industry heads for Florida where the PGA Golf Show takes place. There are just less than 16,000 golf courses in the USA but Florida has more than 1,000 of them, more than any other state. Almost 170,000 Floridians work in the golf industry, so it makes sense that the game's biggest trade fair would find a home here at a time when, elsewhere, the weather's less than ideal.

I'm here to walk the halls and work the lobby and attempt to do some business with the grim and the good. My arranged meetings go well. Everybody's working it, selling tees, selling tee-times, selling holidays. Big-name golfers are selling their course design services. Big-name manufacturers are selling their rocket launchers and missiles. Golf is leisure, certainly, but it makes work for many.

Here in the US, albeit mostly on the other coast, the tech industry is busy making many jobs obsolete, automating life, turning us into information providers for their profitable algorithms. What are we all going to do when nobody needs us? We must work. Golf writers must work. Universal basic income is already being tested in San Francisco and I wonder how

I can sign up; one day, lots of us may have to. The future could be the John Maynard Keynes prediction that economic growth means we work less or it could be a dystopian nightmare of emptiness. Maybe, if it ever comes to it, golf could have a role to play. I'm not certain golf could be the sole cure for homo sapiens' future woes. But it could be one of them. What will people do with their time to find meaning? Musical composition? Growing vegetables? Online game science? Golf course play and maintenance? I'm making it up. But it's a game which generates leisure and labour.

Filling time is one thing, but filling it purposefully is another. Endless surveys mentioned in the endless entrepreneur-type podcasts that I listen to say work must be meaningful for it to be enjoyable, for it to be done well. Happiness comes after meaning. Meaning and motivation leads to happiness, they say. Golf provides some meaning and motivation. We can always learn. We can track scores and statistics. We can improve against ourselves and others. The handicap system makes everyone's efforts relevant, makes the game inclusive. There may not be enough land to go around, but most of us could just hook into our virtual reality simulators and play golf. Perhaps once a month we'd be let out on an actual course. (Surely it won't come to that.) My work is done for the week, but hopefully there'll be more of it before I have to sign up to a statutory common payments system in return for playing computer golf...

The PGA Show is wrapping up and the networking has moved to the Peabody Hotel where I bump into Eoghan O'Connell, someone I've interviewed before about growing up golfing in Killarney, in Ireland. Eoghan lives in Florida these days. The place is packed and we've already made way for a parade of ducks (really, twice a day through the hotel) and now we have to make way for Tom Watson who does a detour and comes over and claps Eoghan on the shoulder. This seals it for me, Eoghan's the man. And then he invites me for a game down at his club, The Fox Club, in Palm City, the following day before I fly for home.

It's a serious course for serious golfers and I'm the least serious amongst them. This is the weekend edition of the twice-weekly individual stableford competition with a skins game thrown in, then a little prizegiving in the bar (no phones and no hats). The winners are announced by the Irish bartender. Club pros from some of the northern states' best clubs are here. This is a no-nonsense place, no tennis courts, no pool, no creche. Almost nobody seems to have a handicap, yet they all tell me Eoghan's the best of the bunch.

It's a remarkable course, tough, really good, really true. The great closing hole is one of those cape holes that's common across the US and uncommon in the UK. It takes some experience playing these holes to learn that, as a less than excellent golfer, they're rarely the place for heroics. The correct approach, on the best of these cape holes – and this is one of them - is that of the Temple of Delphi and its famous motto: nothing in excess. There's no need to take off too much of the angle. It often buys one very little.

Sitting in Eoghan's office after the round and after the prizegiving, he outlines the club's philosophy: rounds well under four hours, good golf, good fun - a purity of approach found more often in Ireland than in America, I'd say.

Across from his desk is a painting of the final hole at Mahony's Point in Killarney, a gift from the members there. "It is my most prized possession in golf," he says.

Eoghan had a truly stunning amateur career, an undefeated member of the Eisenhower Trophy and Walker Cup teams. He played college golf for Wake Forest, Arnold Palmer's alma mater. When he was just 19 he qualified for The Open at Muirfield with a course record 65 at North Berwick on the first day which he then matched the next day. My mind boggles. But his professional career was never as sterling as his younger efforts, a damaged wrist keeping him back and eventually forcing him out of the professional game. But he became a golf industry guy: upscale courses and member clubs and travel groups. "Golf is always good, always has been. It keeps me happy, keeps me gainfully employed," he says.

I tell Eoghan about my friend Alan Grant and the mystery shoes I saw in his car with 'Please Return to The

Fox Club' scrawled on them. "That'd be my writing," says Eoghan. "Alan was here last year and we looked after him."

4 THE OPEN, 4110

Long ago, back in October 1860, the first Open was played at Prestwick on Scotland's west coast. There were just eight players, the game's earliest professionals. They played 36 holes in one day, which is to say three rounds of 12 holes.

Lincoln had not yet become President. Victoria's reign was in its infancy. And there were no more than 20 golf courses on earth, which is to take nothing away from Willie Park Sr who walked away with the prize, a lavish red belt made of Moroccan leather. (It was soon replaced with The Golf Champion Trophy, which we now know as the Claret Jug. It's probably no exaggeration to say that, aesthetically, and perhaps ergonomically - though hell will freeze over before I know that bit for sure - the Claret Jug is the most beautiful of all golf trophies, all sports trophies perhaps. Maybe the old giant European Cup or the tiny Jules Rimet trophies are its equal, but for golfers the jug is the dream.)

The competition returned to Prestwick the following year, 1861, with 10 professionals this time, as well as some amateurs, added to the mix. Old Tom Morris prevailed, his first of four victories. The competition was held at Prestwick 24 times in total. It hosted the first 12 tournaments and then 12 more until 1925, but they don't play it there now. It was replaced by Troon, its very near neighbour. The modern era proved too, well, modern for Prestwick, the crowds too big, the distance gains too great. Yet, if you visited Prestwick today you wouldn't find an outdated wee course. It's not a relic. It's a real challenge for mere mortals and thrilling for anyone of any golfing sensibility. Golf pilgrims should get themselves there, no excuses. The transport links are good. It's right beside the railway station which is basically an obstacle for those playing the first hole. It's right beside the airport too, the only place in the UK where Elvis Presley ever set foot. (And The Kings of the links have all been here, of course.) It became an 18-holer in 1882 and it's still a championship layout, more than hard enough for you and me, more than interesting enough for anyone. But the contemporary golfing athlete, armed and dangerous, would overpower it.

Only the Old Course at St Andrews has hosted The Open more than Prestwick. It's held the tournament on 29 occasions and still does, every five years, almost without fail. An Open at St Andrews is remarkable, when the golf town to end all golf towns is, rightfully, the centre of the sporting world. Actually, the cycling world might have something to say about that, their great race ending on the same day as The Open does. Those men and women - whose numbers are growing and whose legs are as smooth as Sorenstam's swing and who are often blamed with golf's declining numbers as people seek fitness and thrills in preference to a five-mile walk (spoiled) - would say that Paris is the centre of sport on the final Sunday in July when The Tour de France rolls into town.

There are similarities between Le Tour and The Open (at risk of stretching it). Mickelson and Stenson or Nicklaus and Watson exchanging metaphorical punches, going at it beautifully, to-ing and fro-ing, have something in common with those general classification riders trying to get away from one another through sun-dappled woods or up a misty Alpine pass. And in those mountains the crowds get close, right up to the riders, screaming at them, the stench of local wine and barbecued meat on their breath, not so dissimilar to the narrow walkways the golfers navigate to the tees, the smell of beer overwhelming them late in the afternoon. Open crowds used to break free on the Sunday afternoon and past champions have told me about the remarkable odour as they close in all around, basically carrying and jostling their champion up the final hole.

The time trial elements of Le Tour, especially the penultimate day, are 'the race of truth' where there's nowhere to hide, a bit like the final day of a long tournament when the truth will out. The irony is a little laughable, because for all its greatness and European style, cycling is not synonymous with truth whereas, golf, we believe and hope, is an honest game. We play by the rules because we must live with our own conscience, either that or the game doesn't readily lend itself to cheating...

But the classic bike race is typically done and dusted before the first ball is hit in anger on a links course around dawn on a Thursday morning. Normally the cycling's won and lost in the mountains much earlier, almost never on the cobbles of the 8th arrondissement. The 1989 race was only decided when Greg LeMond, an American, was launched down the Champs-Élysées breaking French hearts - because it had been Laurent Fignon's to win - but I only really remember that because it coincided with Greg Norman launching a wood so far, on the fourth playoff hole, Troon's 18th, that he found a previously out-of-reach bunker and handed the tournament, which had been his to win, to Mark Calcavecchia. (I was actually in Paris that day, but I missed the race because I was watching golf on TV! I did though pick up a hat, one of the thousands of freebies handed out by the media sponsor, the capital's newspaper. I wore that hat every day that summer and for a few more to come when I spent time with my French penpal in Burgundy. And even now I imagine there's a little village in France where people would still know me as 'Le Parisien'.)

But anyway, The Open's the thing. Le Tour's glamorous for sure. The Kop in full voice at 2.59pm every other Saturday can be stirring. And people say Louisville on the first Saturday of May is not to be missed. But the final Sunday in July in some out-of-the-way British seaside town is something to behold.

The Open is different to other tournaments. Like the Irish and Scottish Opens which precede it, The British Open Championship (though its organisers prefer it simply be known as The Open) is a three-dimensional affair, played on traditional links courses. More than those events though, the course is always stretched to its maximum, toughened to accommodate the changes in the game. And because it's the oldest Major, players are nervous, dreaming of history and their place in it. Those factors, and the British weather, are all that stands between the greatest of golfers and the most embarrassing of low scores. We all predict a 59 on the Old Course, and the organisers fear it, but thus far it hasn't happened. That sort of number will show up one day. But happily the same player will struggle the next. McIlroy made 63 on day one at St Andrews in 2010, then an 80 the next. That's very McIlroy, very St Andrews, very The Open.

Playing The Open one has to be patient, not just because of the slow play that characterises the professional game, but because on the linksland excellent shots are not always rewarded. This is a test of strength for many modern players. It takes fortitude to wait for luck. The golfer has to find his sense of direction, his special awareness. Yardage charts still count for much and a good caddy will be well worth his fee and percentage, but golfing on seaside courses is like being asked to switch off the satnav and read the map. It's not easy for everyone and it takes practise. You have to visualise where to land the ball and how it will respond to hollows and humps and springy slopes.

International elite golfers must arrive at The Open and, at least on their first visit, see some kind of quaint madness. It's a difficult adjustment for those used to big bright green courses, big cream and bronze hotel rooms. Suddenly the course is anaemic. The skies are muddy brown or battleship grey and the hotel accommodation is often a bizarre British B&B. "Where are you staying?" one American golfer might ask his compatriot. "Oh, in the 1950s," would come the reply.

It was Palmer and then Nicklaus who really reminded reluctant pros they had to attend. Throughout the mid-20th century the small prize fund and the massive travel expense kept the best US golfers at home. The competition was stale. Jones had played earlier in the century, the great amateur. Hogan had made his trip in '53. Others visited. But it was Palmer's win in '59 which made the difference. His charisma and enigmatic stop/start swing, his immense power and notable joy at winning were enough to convince others they should do the same.

Older players, like Old Tom Watson and Old Tom

Morris, can perform and win on this stage. They're out of place on massive lush US courses, but not so here where the ball runs and where acumen can prevail. A number of mature players have come of age at The Open, finally winning a Major late in their career. I think of Roberto de Vicenzo at 44, Darren Clarke at 43. The winner of The Open has been 38 or more 32% of the time since 1990. In the same period, for the other three majors considered together, it's been just 10%. Basically, Open courses are a little shorter than most. And they're now stretched out fully, with little space for further lengthening. The greens are a bit slower as well, to generalise, mostly because of the possibility of high winds. The fairways are firm, but that doesn't play into the hands of the bombers who suddenly find themselves playing into the bunkers. Instead it plays into the hands of the shorter hitters who can run their ball up to ideal driving distance. The big hitters are betwixt and between, messing around with various clubs.

Somehow Open venues lend themselves to the mature approach. On courses where some luck is required it must be hard to play for 72 holes without a major meltdown, a couple of lost balls, a quadruple bogey. It's not concentration, exactly. It's not narrow focus, precisely, not altogether tunnel vision. It's more of an openness, an openness to losing as well as winning. To play your best you must be prepared to lose, ready to accept it. That's the only way you can be free enough to open your shoulders and swing for it. When you close down, fearful of the unfair bounce into the pot bunker, scared of throwing it away, shortening your swing or speeding it up, wishing it was over and you were in the clubhouse with a cute scorecard in hand, then you have no chance. One must be almost happy to lose. Good golfers lose many times. They must accept loss to embrace wins. Maybe that's just easier for the older guys who have already lost so often.

I've loved The Open Championship all my life. It's a less hollow spectacle than many significant sports events. The men in blazers and boring ties who hand out the prizes actually do their bit to keep it real, these Scousers and Glaswegians somehow sounding like high-ranking colonial civil-servants. I'm prepared to accept that having these old duffers running the game is better than having the professionals themselves run it. Then it would all be big money skins-games in the desert, under artificial light, played in luminous Nike shirts, using golf clubs the size of their own heads. (Actually, sounds quite good, in moderation. Maybe they could add heart rate monitors. I always think that would be an interesting innovation for the television audience to enjoy. Who's to say these - or entirely different - changes won't be for the better sometime? A marathon's still a marathon even though Pheidippides was barefoot when he ran the original while today's runners enjoy manned drinks stations and sport shoes with a snappy spring-like energy return he'd have thought might propel him into space.) But the old guard keep the game playable and often the old approach is fairly sound, its methods tried and tested. Probably The Open and The Masters are the pick of the majors because of their closely guarded traditions. Also, perhaps, the lack of sponsor partnerships, or rather the subtlety of them, is key to their high regard. They can be self-satisfied for sure, with much internal branding to remind you where you are (lest you think you're at Ascot or something, an easy mistake to make for the corporate liggers on an endless tour of sporting events on their clients' dime.) But the absence of ubiquitous ads for soft drinks and insurance makes these events more creditable, dependable as well. Advertising reduces prices certainly, but it also reduces the purity of experience. This is very outmoded to say, yet it's surely true that constant advertising interrupts our peace and even ambient advertising plays havoc with our equilibrium. Much of our online lives are experienced free, but look more closely and we are paying with our souls.

The Open does have advertising, but like The Masters, like Wimbledon, the promotional aspects are less in-your-face, more in the back-of-your-mind. There are timepieces everywhere: a well-marketed watchmaker has a sweeping presence at almost all golf events and at The Open its massive clocks keep time and keep watch over every green and tee. These traditional Chinese memento mori should frighten us to keep on keeping on. Time moves fast they tell us. But nobody notices, least of all the players who go about their business at a painful pace.

This sort of level of commercialisation seems just about right. The days of top international golfers spurning the tournament were basically the days of lower prize money so marketing partners are presumably required to keep it relevant. The Open seems to successfully walk the tightrope between commercial realities and an older meaningfulness. The clocks look down on us but when the speeches are made but nobody has to invoke the name of some awful corporation. This keeps our mind on the higher meaning of sport. A bauble can be presented to an amateur and the champion golfer of the year can be declared and we don't have to suffer a commercial break. We can cherish The Open as it always was, kind of.

Like lots of British golfers I look back on a lifetime of Open Championships and I can recall where I was and what the weather was generally like that summer. I can even use them to pinpoint life and times before me.

My sister was born in 1969, not for me the year of the first moon landings. Rather, she was born in the year of a historic triumph at Royal Lytham: a home win for Tony Jacklin. I imagine that this was the dawn of time: giant steps for mankind; Woodstock Festival; The Open broadcast in colour for the first time ever; and a dashing, handsome young winner whose lilac pullover on the last day tells me the conditions were as British as him.

I was born four years later when The Open was at Troon. Of course, I don't remember it. I would have been kept safely indoors, just a few miles up the coast. The weather was so atrocious new born babies couldn't have left home for fear of drowning. Lee Trevino was seeking his third consecutive Open victory that summer. He didn't make it. I guess he'd used up all his luck the previous year, holing pitches from everywhere, even when it looked like he wouldn't win and that he'd given up. No, in 1973 it was Tom Weiskopf who came through, a well-deserved win for the tall guy, the great player with the fiery temper. It would be his only major and, therefore, close to his heart. He made his mark as a player in Scotland. And he came back many years later to make his mark as an architect, laying out the lovely course at Loch Lomond.

In 1975 Tom Watson broke his duck following two US national championships which he really ought to have won. He had to dig deep on a windy final day to produce a level par round. And on the Sunday playoff – the last of the 18-hole play-offs, tournaments then mostly finishing regulation play on a Saturday – he fought through more wind and rain and the toughest closing stretch in championship golf to finish one under and win by a shot. I never think of Carnoustie without some rain. (I never visit it without some rain.)

Then I think of 1977. (Everyone thinks of 1977.) I wasn't there but I imagine I was: mixed, quite windy weather on the West of Scotland; people drinking Tennent's lager from cans; tartan tammies galore; and wide flares aplenty. And then a day of wonderful sunshine and wonderful golf, the much-vaunted Duel in The Sun. Tom and Jack shot matching consecutive 68s, 70s, 65s and then, in the final round, Tom made yet another 65, this time to Jack's 66. The coup de theatre came on the 72nd hole when Jack slashed a do-or-die drive into deep rough but somehow, miraculously, just found the green with his second. Tom was lying almost stone dead in two, but Jack somehow, impossibly, holed his colossal putt. Tom now faced the longest short birdie putt ever, but he holed it and the gladiators embraced and all was good with the world.

Seve's win in '84 at St Andrews was perhaps the first time I watched televised golf. Seve won three Opens but the first one was his favourite, everybody's favourite, certainly, my favourite. His long putt on the final green hesitated on the lip of the hole before dropping and setting off his celebration, a joyous moment. Dave Cannon, the great golf photographer, framed the iconic shot. He was greenside and captured the Spaniard, fist clenched. 'Il Momento,' Ballesteros called it, and he had it tattooed on his arm. It was probably that Open which made me think I should be playing golf. The leaderboard for the final day was full of the best players in the world at the time. That day Ballesteros beat Bernhard Langer, Tom Watson, Fred Couples, Lanny Wadkins, Nick Faldo, and Greg Norman.

In 1990 I was actually, finally, at St Andrews with great friends Arnaud, Iain and Stephen. I remember watching Faldo on the range, the calm centre, the hurricane about him. He was wonderful, metronomic, dropping wedges onto the same spot again and again. No wonder he won by a mile. It was good weather too. We stayed in a caravan. I got drunk on a hideous liqueur. We went swimming. I kissed some poor girl.

1995 was a warm summer. I'd graduated and was spending a luxurious couple of months seeking work but really relaxing with friends, from Kilconquhar in the east to Southend in the west. I remember watching the last day's golf at Sarah's house in the Glasgow suburbs, a few of us lying around probably wearing 90s fashions, drinking sugary fizzy drinks and maybe even smoking cigarettes, a bit like John Daly who would win despite Rocca's great escape through the Valley of Sin.

All Scotsmen remember 1999. The rain. Carnoustie. And then triumph and joy.

All Frenchmen probably remember it too. The rain. Carnoustie. And then a fiasco and failure.

Van de Velde was foolish. But we feel sorry for him. Not all sportsmen, in the heat of the moment, can be Jake LaMotta in Raging Bull seeing everything in slow motion. Things went too fast for Jean and the title got away from him while Paul Lawrie, a Scotsman, put together an extraordinary 22 holes. We were there, Richie, Ross, Tony and I, in the grandstand on the right side of the 18th, the one Van de Velde hit. We were soaked by endless drizzle. Tony almost slapped the very drunk college kid behind us who kept shouting about how he'd see us at the Justin Leonard celebration party later. But Leonard didn't come through and we got a home win and sang Flower of Scotland in the rain. Frenchmen are meant to win The Tour de France, Scotsmen The Open. I remember Lawrie's final approach shot, his ball forever in the air through the wind and rain carrying the hopes of a small nation!

The next year Tiger, through mist and low cloud, shredded the field, writing his name in history (again), this time as the winner of the millennial Open at the Home of Golf, the victor by a distance, the greatest of them all. (In most sports we like parity, close competition. In golf, for some reason, we quite enjoy domination. Faldo walking it. Woods walking it. The front-runner who holds on is impressive. The one who goes from strength to strength is doubly so.)

And on it goes: my first child was born – slightly inauspiciously I have to say – in the year Todd Hamilton won at Troon. But the weather was very good. My second child was born when Harrington won his first of two Opens and I remember umbrellas at

Carnoustie. It was a terrible summer when Clarke prevailed four years later. But it was scorchio when Mickelson won at Muirfield, the fairways like runways of burnt stubble and my feet aching after following that famous final round. I watched Mickelson tackling those 18 holes of elaborate brilliance which he more than lived up to. I'm sure he had almost no intention of going where that course and that tournament led him.

Almost all golf tournaments are enjoyable for the spectator. Goodwill generally abounds and we, the fans, live out the shots we see. We have favourite players, but we don't really mind who wins, apart from the occasional patriotic moment. We walk the courses, tracking Spieth or Garcia, channeling Jones or Ballesteros. We walk the same ground as the greats. We imagine we're in it together, save for a few ropes. And yet, the golfers are alone. They fashionably talk in plural pronouns, the 'we' referring to them and their caddies. But really they're just being generous. It's a forlorn career-calling, a precarious high-wire-act to be performed solo and at the same time in front of countless strangers. The golfer's career choice is like that of the long-form novelist but with money in the bank.

Actually, they're not all rolling in it. There's no draft, no contracts (well, endorsements I suppose). If you're injured you're not earning. Only a tiny number of players make money from the game compared to soccer, baseball, basketball, football, cricket even. Sure,

200 people make big money. But that's it. You can make a living teaching the game, arranging golf trips, being an agent. But it's just a chosen few who make money playing it and they have to perform.

Through the years, sat in a grandstand beside the first, listening to the official starter, Ivor Robson, now retired, announcing players onto the tee with that distinct upward inflection, I've marvelled at the outward calm of these players. Ivor's voice, reassuring to spectators, must be frightening to those whose moment has arrived. (I've also marvelled at the steely resolve of Ivor who, throughout The Open, has a sandwich and a glass of water at 7pm each evening, nothing more all week lest he be forced to leave his post. He loses 14 lbs – a stone – during the week. He should patent a diet.)

We may occasionally think – when we see pro golfers wearing their caps indoors and talking a steady-stream of cliché – that these men are untroubled by complexity, strangers to subtlety. But see them hold their nerve in the tense moments that abound at Open Championships and it becomes clear that they have some special mental reserves. The cortex is where rational thought takes place while the thalamus is the seat of the emotions. These must be aligned, or perhaps overridden, to play golf well at the highest level. In July the winner accomplishes this across four of the most intense days conceivable to any golfer.

Golf reveals much. Even over nine holes played alone as the shadows lengthen one can learn much about their inner nature. But four full rounds played in the spotlight reveals almost all there is to know about the player. At The Open, with its many distractions and special significance, the winner performs a miracle and rightly earns a small place in history for his efforts.

5 ROAD INCIDENT, 5140

E choes of the past. Souls of golfers dead and gone. This old town is haunted, full of ghosts, full of ghost-hunters too. The ghosts are those of Allan Robertson, Bobby Jones, Seve Ballesteros, anyone who was anyone in the game. The paranormal investigators are international tourists, here to soak up golf's past and to play the courses which are museum pieces, but also living, breathing, changing championship challenges, still used by the world's best players as they compete for great prizes, once every five years for The Open Championship itself.

In the popular imagination, as well as in the communications campaigns of those who promote the place, this is The Home of Golf. And that should be good enough for all of us. The weavers of Dirleton and the fishwives of Musselburgh might see things differently. And others who knocked a pebble around elsewhere on Scotland's east coast might have something to say about it. But St Andrews is it, Ground Zero: the golfer's Mecca. Written records show the game being played here in 1552, so we can assume even earlier beginnings.

Courses worldwide are named after this little place, from Newfoundland to New York to New Zealand (and points in between, but the alliteration appealed).

Golfers fantasize about playing here. American men, in their 50s and 60s mostly, some lucky younger ones perhaps, come here to realise a dream, to check off an item on the bucket-list. They are pilgrims in their tech spec golf clothes by day, large fit chinos and shirts by night, friends together, many drinks down. Occasionally American visitors bring their wives as well. "Hey Ted, touch the turf", I've heard called out as an American lady made it to the first tee just ahead of her husband, bending down to feel the grass. It's sacred ground for many. Edward Thomas, an English poet, was once asked by Robert Frost why he volunteered in 1915. His answer was to pick up some English soil and let it slip through his fingers. Similarly, there are people today who're ready to fight for The Old Course. When changes to it are announced many get up in arms, though it's a course which has been forever tampered with, kept fit for purpose.

Northern European visitors also come here in decent numbers. These rangy, handsome guys - with swings so sharp it seems impossible they're not tour pros - often travel with partners too, beautiful women who dutifully walk the fairways with their sporting spouse or who sometimes don expensive rainwear and play along as well. It's often mistakenly said that because the blonde gene is regressive the last natural blonde will walk the earth, only a couple of hundred years hence, somewhere on the Scandinavian Peninsula. But for now there seems to be an endless supply of blondes visiting this eastern outpost.

A Finnish fourball, say, plus wives and caddies, is 12 people. That's serious. It might as well be the entourage of an Open Championship tee time with players, caddies, families, agents, media, referees, scoreboard carriers and quiet-please sign holders, like a Roman legion marching into battle. They hit glorious tee shots and stroll off down the fairway, embarking on one of the slowest rounds in Scotland.

The tall Europeans rarely make a mistake off the first, mostly splitting the fairway with their three wood. I don't know how they do it. Playing an important shot – and this one is salient for most golfers - we finally feel what we know from science, that the earth is travelling at dizzying speeds, spinning and hurtling through space. Suddenly the ground is moving; everything swims around us. But these guys are unfazed.

North Americans - chief amongst the visiting golfers – rarely miss either. They've come to a foreign country but their confidence is such that they make it their own. There's long been an historic bond between Scottish invention and American leisure, be it whisky, telephones, televisions, highways or, in this case, fairways. They seem to like it, standing on the tee. We all dream of being adored on stage, appreciated finally. Well, here on the first tee is a chance to show the world what we're made of and the Americans almost never get it wrong.

But it doesn't go well for all. Every day there will be a few shockers. People come and stand on this tee and, sometimes for the first time, they confront themselves properly. Of course, experience and skill are the real factors, but accomplished players sometimes wilt here. Public executions no longer exist in Scotland. But this is close. The first tee is just 50 yards from the Martyrs' Monument, which was actually the old first tee. The monument commemorates those burned at the stake in St Andrews for reading the Bible in English and advocating married clergy. The old religion could be ferocious, the new religion too. And the game of golf, a religion to many, has its own cruel and unusual punishments.

A decent sized slice of life plays down this hole. Some are nervous. Some are cool. Some are big-game hunters here to bag another golf course. I imagine, maybe unfairly, that they don't see the ghosts. Others are reverential, the searchers, more sensitive to their surrounds perhaps.

Sizable crowds gather, watching the jet set players faff around and hand things to their caddies. Eventually we are rewarded with some golf shots. It reminds us how little of this game is pure action and how much of it is simply foreplay. We're also reminded that the distance between a good shot and a bad shot can be 200 yards but can also be millimetres, nanoseconds.

Sometimes it's less traumatic to look left to the 18th. The golfers, admittedly tiring after their counter clockwise pilgrimage round The Old Course, are playing smoothly now, putting out with some aplomb on the fabulous final green before heading off for a shave and shower and to perform some animal sacrifice or at least eat a burger and drink deeply in The Jigger Inn or Dunvegan Hotel. No pint of beer ever went down hard in these places following a never-to-be-forgotten game on this ancient links.

The 18th green is a thing of beauty, an end in itself, literally and artistically. It's the handiwork of Old Tom Morris. It's huge, sloping and spectacular, a fitting monument to the man who simply, utterly and without any whatevers, is the most important person in the history of golf. He's the man who created the modern game. He was also a scab and a blackleg, an early supporter of golfing technology and distance improvement equipment, the stuff that modern life is made of.

Tom Morris was born in 1821 in St Andrews, back when golf was a provincial pursuit, specific to Scotland, specific really to its east coast. He died in 1908, truly Old Tom, age 87. By modern standards his personal life had been tragic: he had outlived his wife and children. But by anyone's standards it had been remarkable. His progress had been Dickensian, from poor and uneducated to celebrated and feted by all society. He became globally famous, as did golf. Tom Morris rose up in the world and so did his favourite game. One couldn't have happened without the other.

Like every other kid in St Andrews, Tom was golfing, or something like it, around the streets and maybe around the links from an early age. He probably caddied too. And when he was 14 he became apprentice to Allan Robertson, a distant relative and close family friend, the town's first golf professional, therefore the world's first golf professional, also Scotland's acknowledged finest golfer, the first man to break 80 on The Old Course, Tom soon becoming the second.

Tom was Allan's assistant for 15 years. When he wasn't stuffing a top hat full of feathers into a small sewn leather pouch to make a featherie golf ball, or assisting in early course designs, he was partnering Allan in various challenge games, the world's greatest two players, never beaten off scratch. Featherie balls were their livelihood. Sizable winnings from complex matches organised with gambling gentlemen golfers were their dividends and pension pot. These matches garnered considerable newspaper column inches. When they were played between St Andrews professionals and those from across the water in East Lothian the media hype was greater still, the wagers inflating as well.

In 1851 Allan fired Tom when he found him accidentally endorsing new technology. Improbably, Tom had lost his supply of featheries and his playing partner gave him a gutta ball to try. Playing back into the town – we must imagine this on the shared 1st and 18th fairways, the greatest of golfing arenas – Tom's group met Allan's heading out onto the links. Allan was told that Tom was playing well with a new fangled ball. Three hours later Tom was dismissed. Allan was a traditionalist, a luddite perhaps, but also a businessman. He organised protests against the new imported gum. But soon Allan's ball-making business was dead. And soon golf, already growing steadily on the east coast with clubs being formed from north to south, would explode across Scotland and, in line with British Empire building, the world. The new improved and affordable golf ball made it possible. Tom had been disloyal, but the mighty march of Victorian progress could not be stopped by anyone. He was a young man, presumably interested in hitting the ball further and straighter, perhaps not so different from those in thrall to the output of research & development golf labs in Southern California now. For golf, this was the Big Bang. It was Elvis recording That's Alright at Sun Records, except grown women didn't get giddy about the gutta-percha golf ball, despite its cleaner lines and improved performance in the wet.

Following this incident, the Morris family spent almost 15 years in Prestwick, on the other side of the country, where Old Tom built the famous course and his son, a genuine golfing genius, learned the game. When they returned to St Andrews it was so that the father of the game could settle into 40 years as Keeper of the Green, a role specially created by The Royal & Ancient Golf Club which saw him improve and formalise the course, perfect the greenkeeping techniques still used today and generally grow into his position as the grand old man of golf.

It was Tom who struck the opening shot in the inaugural Open Championship and went on to win it four times. Young Tom, his son, also won the event four times.

When Old Tom died he was afforded a grand funeral and was eulogised around the globe. He was buried in the grounds of the town cathedral next to Young Tom who had died in 1875, just 24 years old. Allan Robertson's grave is nearby too.

Old Tom's death had finally come when he stumbled and fell down stairs in The New Club. Despite his preeminent status in the game Tom was never a member of The R&A. They had been generous employers, remunerating him well and continuing to do so when he was nominally retired. But he was, after all, a weaver's son. The New Club, though, was his. The chair where he sat – Dead Man's Chair – and the magnifying glass he used to look out on the links in his last years, are still there, perfectly preserved.

Sitting in that chair, taking visits from the great and the good, watching the comings and goings on the links through his eye-glass, Old Tom was looking at the future: an increasingly popular game played internationally over a standardised 18 holes on courses which were all based on the one he had refined with his bare hands, tearing out gorse bushes and piling on sand.

That St Andrews had settled on 18 holes is a matter of complete chance. 18 holes, it was deemed in the mid-18th century, improved the course. 18, it appears, for playability reasons specific to the land, simply worked better than 22.

So, 18 became the universal golfing number and by happy coincidence it's also the magic number of Major Championships won by the game's great exponent, Jack Nicklaus, the number all other pretenders dream about.

King James IV of Scotland, the first named golfer in history, made 18 pilgrimages to the shrine of St Duthac which stands beside what is now the Old Tom Morris-designed links at Tain, from where, across the Firth, one can see that other sacred site, Royal Dornoch.

Outside of golf it carries some weight too. James Joyce's Ulysses has 18 chapters and arguably no book has more structural significance. Shakespeare's most famous sonnet, the only one which might be read as a paean to the game, goes by the number 18. It's also the number of years missing from Jesus' biblical biography, the time he spent with The Buddha, or visiting Glastonbury, or golfing in Scotland, or perhaps just taking a fishing trip with some girls from The Church of The Nazarene. It depends which crazies you subscribe to.

And 18 is the Hebrew number for life, at least it is when gematria, the numerology system which assigns numerical values to words and phrases, is employed. In any case, 18 is considered propitious in Judaism. Also, 18 is the only number that equals twice the sum of its decimal digits. Maybe mathematicians get a kick out of that. It's probably beautiful. (1+8 = 9; 9x2 = 18.) So an 18 hole course is, by accident and not design, of no small substance.

Perhaps though the Society of St Andrews Golfers, back in 1764 before they were regal and old, missed a trick. Almost two centuries after their monumental decision a clever book publisher decided that a novel should be called Catch-22, not Catch-18 as its author Joseph Heller had intended. The reasons aren't entirely clear but the reviews were good and the sales stupendous.

There's more magic though in the configuration of the holes themselves than in their overall number. The Old Course, in its order of pars, is a palindrome, the same backwards as forwards. There are others, but the odds of any course being palindromic are something like 1/17,536, so it's strange – and splendid – that The Old Course has this distinction. Real things tend not to be perfectly ordered, real lives all being imperfect. Yet The Old Course is built to a perfect pattern which is accidental. Such fearful symmetry, in a novel or film, would be struck out by a good editor as distracting and unbelievable. At St Andrews the improbable pattern is part of the fascination, a secret code surely, a lost meaning...

Certainly, it's enough to inspire someone to write an over-zealous golf book with some acrostical significance crammed into its chapter headings and first lines. They might call that book, rather grandly and ponderously perhaps, The Meaning of Golf. They might even pace out its 18 chapters in the same way as The Old Course is laid out. Yet for all that effort and pleasure the game will surely, always, be endlessly, gloriously, futile, a futility which will be further demonstrated to me in about eight hours' time.

I'm drinking whisky in a St Andrews hotel. Story of my life. But this is a good hotel and the whisky's great. It's three in the morning and we've been on the strong stuff for half a day. We're guests of a Scottish whisky distiller, a Major championship sponsor, The Spirit of The Open. We've been golfing. We've been whiskied and wined and dined. Dr Bill Lumsden, their mad scientist of a master blender, the Willy Wonka of whisky-making, has led us through some serious tasting. We've been drinking champagne on the balcony of The R&A with Tony Jacklin. It's been glorious and instructive and boozy. Tomorrow morning we play The Old Course and some unusual good sense is now telling me – too late admittedly – to get to bed.

We are a few golf media types and I'm a hanger-on. Eventually I take my own advice and head upstairs, leaving the stylish Swedish journalist, the last man lolling, at the bar. He's in my group tomorrow, the first ones out on the course. Hopefully he's not my partner.

I'm asleep or passed out instantly, not for me the wel-ter of worries experienced in St Andrews' many bed and breakfasts, the fitful sleeps before golfers' dates with destiny.

In the morning I make it to town with time to spare. But reversing my rental car into a comfortably large space on The Scores I feel a violent lurch, hear a colos-sal crash. The front bumper is lying on the road. I've clipped a raised pavement. I abandon it. There'll be time later to hopefully have it repaired before I make for Edinburgh airport. I try not to think about the £1200 excess insurance payment.

I buy some Irn Bru (Scotland's Other National Drink), gifts for the Swede and German in my group. I get bottles of water for myself and the other Scotsman. Somehow they're all there waiting for me. The Swede looks broken but the German golf journalist and the eminent Scottish sports writer are fine. It's to be Scotland versus Mainland Europe, one drunk and one sober man apiece. The Scots are excited because it's a crystal clear and quickly warming winter morning, but we're more excited for our continental cousins playing here for the first time.

Light pours through the upper windows of Ayai Sofia in Istanbul. Smiling children skate beside the Rockerfeller Centre in New York at Christmas. The Aurora Boreallis lights up the northern night sky. A solstice sunrise splits the central columns of Stonehenge. But forget all that. This is as good as it gets: St Andrews, the Old Course, first tee, first thing.

There are no first tee nerves or no time for them anyway. No crowds gather. We play away from the town out onto the links with plenty of pars between us. It's fabulous to be out there on the hallowed ground, nobody before us and nobody behind.

The view back to the town is pleasing. It's a medieval huddle of a place even in the 21st Century, Scotland's equivalent of Urbino. The University, a grand affair, is the oldest in the country.

St Andrews was, for a long time, the centre of clerical life in Scotland too. The town heaves with pointed arches, architectural breakthroughs which came out of the east, just as golf itself would. The many spires are a spectacular backdrop.

In the foreground the imposing building of The R&A Clubhouse is actually one of the less ancient structures in town. It's where rules are made and maintained, the rules of golf which grow on you the more you know of them. As an institution it's hard to love, reactionary in the extreme. As a building it's imperfect, though stoic and Scottish. As a moral idea it's not so bad. I mean, last night I was ready to become a member if they'd have me. Presumably they never will. But I consider the town's motto: Dum Spiro Spero, or, While I Breathe I Hope.

But forget all that. I'm playing well. I'm full of whisky and I love this place. Sure, it's a racket and visitors will leave with their wallets considerably lighter than when they arrived. But it's got charm. I think maybe I should live here, move the family up to Scotland. No doubt real estate is costly. Certainly there's a lot of cashmere on show. But it's a very real place, very liveable, not Noho or Notting Hill, just a wonderful wee town dedicated to golf.

OK, back to reality, or maybe not reality because the Scots, it appears, are three up against serious opposition, low single figure foreigners. We're just dunting it down the fairway but they're hitting it sure and far like professionals. No matter though because, on paper we're all over them, three up after five.

I ask them how they learned to play so well, imagining their grim European childhoods with just one golf course to every million people... It turns out they took lessons. "Craig, in Sweden if you want to do something you learn to do it properly." This is a revelation to me. I keep thinking about it, that and the

£1200 excess. Lessons, eh? My partner and I have had five lessons between us and I had all of them. We don't look like much, but the gap's growing. We're now four up and I reckon I'm just one over par.

I'm liking this, the mediocre Jock golfers putting significantly better opponents to the sword, like maybe we know something about the game's ancient mysteries. We don't. But we've both got good short games.

Out here at the turn, on nine and ten, the course is fairly featureless. For all its manicuring, this is an elemental course. Historic golf courses have a charm that speaks to those who will listen I think, self-righteously, as the whisky works wonders and I make another par.

Are our international guests wondering if this is even a proper golf course? It doesn't really look like one out here. It gives lie to that catch-all subjective statement, I know it when I see it. Famously, that applies to pornography, but it doesn't work with a fabulous golf course, because The Old Course doesn't, exactly, look like one. Yet it is. It's truly fabulous.

My game's unravelling a little. On 14, in Hell bunker, I'm reminded that overall in life our predicament seems hopeless but we somehow find a way. I manage a bogey. My partner makes par. The match is over. We've won, five and four. I begin to think a little of my own scorecard which is looking far tidier than expected.

The last few drives have been pokes, just holding onto the fairways. The Road hole is nearing. A caddy would be hiding the driver from me about now.

An obstacle, seen clearly, should be an inspiration. Seen by someone with doubts, someone with something to lose, someone with a hangover, well then it becomes a hindrance. The hotel and the sheds below it, the ones you're meant to drive straight over, they're looming large.

We're all having a fine old time but I'm thinking too hard. I'm somehow still just two over when we reach 17. I've been carrying a spare ball in my pocket all this time, like a worry stone. I'd not noticed it, being bundled up, wearing winter gloves. But I realise now that I've been rolling it over in my hand walking the last few holes. It seems I'd already made a decision about this famous drive.

The greatest of great golf holes lies in front of me. A large hotel beckons and unexpectedly its car park beyond it. I can only apologise to the various Bentley and Jaguar owners staying there. The slice was significant, let's say.

You know, I was stood there with one of those big-headed drivers in my hand and Old Tom would have been turning in his grave, not because of the club so much as the architectural disgrace that is the hotel (and that's an indictment from a dead Scottish Protestant). Anyway, I've got this big driver thing - not as big as the really big ones because I'm a man of principle but it's only a decade out of date - and my mind's racing and, like I say, Old Tom wouldn't have worried about the golf club because he was the guy who started it all with gutta percha. So, I'm all over the place and I begin my swing... I begin my swing like a 25 handicapper on mind altering drugs (you know who you are.)

Nobody's trying to tackle me. Nobody's running at me. I'm under no threat. There's no external pressure. There's only internal pressure and I bend to it and I break.

I was in uncharted waters, a decent scorecard in my pocket for the most meaningful of all courses. What could go wrong? Nothing short of a calamity equal to the meteor that wiped out the dinosaurs, that's all.

It's called choking, a term which perhaps originated in Salem when those under suspicion, their lives at stake, couldn't swallow a Holy Communion wafer, the test for witchcraft. Maybe there's a better German compound word for what's just happened. It's probably 40 or 50 letters long and cleverly encompasses the whisky, the car, the unseasonal sunshine, the reputation of the 17th and a powerful need to self-destruct denying oneself the possibility of personal glory. It probably hints at what should be learned but what we know we will never really learn. But if the German knows such a word he's not saying it. He's just looking shocked. (I guess it's the first time we've played together so he's not familiar with my work.) The Swede tells me how sorry he is, that he's loved watching my score come together and is sad to see it disappear. The Scottish sports writer is pitilessly observant. "There are a few lessons in that," he says. "Mind you, I've never seen anything like it."

There's a lesson about whisky and golf, how maybe they don't mix in quantity (and today is a day to quit drinking, for a day anyway). There's something about pride and falls and the order they come in. Everything else we know about golf is here too: the need for a steady head both externally and internally, that one must let go of expectations. Maybe there's some good to be taken from it and that to par home would have been too much, that I'd somehow get the wrong idea. An easy ride is not what golf's about, the wise Scottish sports writer reckons. He's right. I'm reminded of the toast given by the fictional golf pro Shivas Irons who says to beware the quick sands of golfing improvement, that the thing is to enjoy ourselves: "I say fuck oor ever getting better".

Famously, slightly repetitively, golf is a four-letter word. It has once again demonstrated to me the sinful pride of human nature. It's ego-cleansing. As we know from the story of Adam and Eve, without transgressions there can be no knowledge. And on this trip I've transgressed, but have I gained any knowledge? I mean, I'm sure I've done this before. I can't quite remember all the places. My scores aren't recorded for posterity like those on the PGA Tour. But I've had these feelings. I've definitely compromised as many decent rounds as I have closed them out. This might just be Hegel's aphorism in practise: that all we learn from history is that we never learn from history.

I got in my own way, mechanically I mean, but also metaphorically. I should have taken the time to catch my breath, to learn to breathe. But I forgot. Golf courses are a good place to catch up on breathing.

Honestly, I can't tell you how it didn't all end with more whisky and a revolver in a darkened room. But this is golf's magic: it keeps you coming back. The game is tragi-comic, in my case with the emphasis on the former.

We had our Bannockburn on the 14th green, an agreeable victory for the underdogs. But I have a feeling I've turned today into a loss, my Mons Graupius or Flodden or Culloden. I hit a perfectly good second tee shot, ok anyway, a bit of a fearful pull down the left side. Then I nudge my approach into The Road bunker. I manage to get out and onto the green, clearing the face that wrecked a thousand shots. And I shakily took three putts, making an eight, a quadruple bogey.

The denouement must be a par so I can be sure that a lesson has been learned. But no, I finish with a double bogey. I had been taught a lesson and then I was taught it again, and now I must try to understand it.

We have fond farewells on the great 18th green, perched above The Valley of Sin. I make calls and find a bodyshop on the hill above town. I drive the car there, the bumper tied to the bonnet. It'll take a few hours, which luckily I have. It'll cost a few hundred pounds, and luckily I have a credit card. I walk back into St Andrews, through the cathedral grounds, a quick visit to some famous last resting places, then off for a sandwich in the sunshine, some quiet recuperation while I wait for the rental car to be reassembled.

The perfect round, that rarity, is a great thing. You can learn from it, learn how to do it again if you're lucky. But one can also learn from bad rounds, from mistakes. The mistakes are guaranteed. Our fragility is always there and we must live with it almost all the time. I'm in love with golf partly because it doesn't reciprocate my feelings. It has jilted me on many a tee.

I'm already over my errors, ready to make them again or better still avoid them. Either way I'm happy to have had a meaningful morning on The Old Course.

Why is The Old Course so good? It's not just historical snobbery, sentimentality. It's the favourite course of countless great golfers, the greatest golfers even. I believe it's as good as those experts say because it's not overdone. Because of the character of the people who first played it the course demonstrates restraint. It hasn't been bungled, yet. Old Tom didn't dig a pond. For sure, the course has almost always been there, just lying there, but it's not like the land is astonishing. The course became astonishing over the years as man

– one man in particular – worked it hard but worked it subtly.

In the Scottish way of things its logic was never aesthetic, so it's entirely by chance that some of it should be so charming, that the 11th should be so perfect, that the first and 18th should be so lovely, backing into the town. Considered together they are great holes, so easy yet sometimes so hard. It's also entirely typical that the hotel on the 17th should be such a sprawling 1960s scar on this precious historic landscape.

All courses worldwide are an approximation of The Old Course. All are, in a small way, a reminder of it. So, in coming here all golfers should feel, a little, at home.

Like the best things in life, The Old Course is both simple and complex. The Old Course has not yet finished saying what it has to say.

6 UNFAIR SPLENDOURS, 3600

Is golf the greatest game in the world? Many would say so. But then, golf has truly excellent propaganda.

Almost all golfers watch The Masters. At least for a few hours we all tune in: same time, same place. In this way, every year, the game's aesthetics, its incredible difficulty and its pleasant surface manners are enforced worldwide. This rite of spring serves to spread the message that golf is something to aspire to: a beautiful pursuit for gentlemen of improbable skills.

It's a meaningful moment in the calendar, marking, for golfers, a new beginning as surely as the solstice did for Pagans or as Easter might for Christians. And the CBS output from Augusta National is as tightly controlled as any sermon the Catholic Church might sanction for its great events.

The broadcast values might feel dated, a strangely saturated sensation of ultra-high-definition images and unreal colour schemes. And the advertising from just a limited number of selected sponsors is trying, as if a lack of variety is somehow better. But the over-all feeling is – as intended – one of tradition: a tradition unlike any other they say, over and over again, so that even Joseph Goebbels would admire the repetition.

It's April. Augusta's wonders are on display. The voice of the final four has his vocal chords in tune. The schmaltz and the golf can begin.

In Spain thoughts turn to Ballesteros and Olazabal, perhaps Sergio Garcia too. In Canada they think of Mike Weir, in Argentina Ángel Cabrera. In Australia it should be Adam Scott but they can't help thinking of Greg Norman and the collapse he suffered at the hands of that automaton pom, Sir Nick Faldo, who they're thinking of in England.

Around the world golfers measure out their years in Sunday broadcasts of blooming flowers and dyed-blue waters, unimaginably green greens, grown men praying as they walk across stone bridges built by German prisoners of war and named after the legends of the game, grown men crying as they succumb to terrible pressures or else fulfil fantasies of greatness. In the southern States the weather is kind. In the northern zones, in Europe as well, this warm week-end in Georgia inspires us to get the clubs out of the garage and begin to live the dream for another season.

We all love The Masters and its great arena. For sure, it's a holier-than-thou, hillier-than-it-looks-on-television, over-long, over-grown indigo plantation turned plant nursery turned golf course which has been set up for left-handed bombers. But we are in awe. All that snobbery and sexism, all that racism and rigidity, those choking yellow clouds of pine pollen drifting over the course: yet it's good; it's great; it's really great.

Easy to say when just spectating, but the course looks almost manageable with fairly fat fairways and appealing driving lines. No illusions though, this course is long and low scoring requires brilliance playing into the greens and putting on them too. The ordinary player would struggle to hit and hold them, would breathe fast and shallow over most short putts. The crowds stand and gawp and make strange noises as balls land, seemingly stop, then start to slide, picking up pace and spinning away. The greens have to be read from distance, they say, memorised too. It's a subtle affair. And stimping at around 14 it's also a bit of a pantomime. Every putt is an attempted lag putt. But golfers are, to varying degrees, sophisticated. When they started to make the greens really really fast here there were endless complaints. They're like glass. Unplayable by the weekend. They need water. But now it's accepted. Augusta is a ferocious challenge and many perfect and pure strikes are required to win here.

The course has always been tinkered with. But when changes were made they were mostly gentle, a little lengthening here and there. And when they were severe they were inspired: most obviously the replacement of the old Bermuda greens with bentgrasses for the 1981 tournament when we began to feel the need for speed.

In general though, the antediluvian Augusta was shorter and slower. Like most courses it was forever being amended, but never drastically. Then came the flood: a person of colour who smashed the course to smithereens in 1997, playing a game Jack Nicklaus probably didn't recognise, which is to echo the words Bobby Jones had said about Nicklaus himself back in 1965.

The Augusta powers had already humanely altered the course to protect it from that big-boned boy from Ohio who was powerful in the extreme. The bunkers on the left of the closing hole, for example, were put there because Jack was battering it up that side. With Tiger though they had to change the whole thing, stretch it out on the rack and radically revise it. More pines were introduced. A 'first cut' of rough appeared beside the fairways. Tees were pushed way back. An argument says that simply played into the strong hands of the big-hitters because the fairways don't narrow and disappear at long driving length the way they often do elsewhere. It meant the big-guys simply wind up and hit it out to their maximum distance. But distance defines much of the game now. So Augusta – in this way – is very progressive.

It is the crucible of course architecture. Every year they get the world's greatest golfers down below the Mason-Dixon line and they see what they can do to the course. Then they spend the next twelve months adjusting it to stop them doing it next time. The changes made each year since 1997 have been profound. And the club itself - ostensibly a separate entity from the tournament – has changed too. It has changed to accommodate the modern world as well as its great new champion.

The modern world wasn't a consideration when Clifford Roberts, the farmboy turned investment banker, and Bobby Jones, the great amateur gentleman, conceived Augusta.

They invited Dr Alister Mackenzie, a course architect whose work they'd admired at Pasatiempo and Cypress Point, to plan the course. They didn't pay him what they promised and he died in straitened circumstances.

In 1932, as work on the course came to an end, Mackenzie wrote Roberts a letter. "I've not been paid a cent since last June, and we have mortgaged everything we have." He begged for five hundred dollars "to keep us out of the poor house." A $10,000 fee had been agreed to design the course. But this was reneged on during construction and the sum was halved. In the end, even that bill wasn't settled.

Roberts and Jones envisioned something timeless, invented instant traditions and realised a fantasy of an ultra-exclusive enclave that the world could enjoy glimpses of through the tournament they created. And to go with all that they got the ultimate course layout for just $2,000, the total sum that they paid Mackenzie.

It was Roberts who vowed that as long as he was alive the golfers would be white and the caddies black. As financial advisor to Eisenhower it seems he illegally channelled public funds to the Republicans. He defaulted on the building costs of Augusta so the club could re-organise and trade debt-free under a new name. Latterly he banned Jones from Masters' prize-giving ceremonies because he was wheelchair bound. Roberts was, by most accounts, an introvert with a passion for power and a lust for money. Then in 1977, age 83, he shot himself in the head with a Smith & Wesson .38, out on the par-3 course. Couldn't happen to a nicer guy someone might think. But really it's just a sad story. He killed himself because he had terminal cancer. His parents before him had both killed themselves. So we continue with fantasies. He was an ethno-centric racist and a bully because of circumstances, because of the time and the place.

Anyway, the man's dead and despite remaining as chairman in memoriam, non-white members were allowed into Augusta for the first time in 1990, non-black caddies seven years before that.

Women wanted in on the act too, wouldn't you know? They protested: it's the 21st century and this is unacceptable. The club protested: we're just a bunch of guys enjoying golf and cigars, a few money games away from the wives. But one woman in particular, Martha Burk, wasn't buying it. Augusta is a powerful cabal which legitimises sexism at the highest levels, she claimed. So, Burk, President of The National Council of Women's Organizations based in Washington, decided to stand up to them. Well, she sent them a letter and the unhappy club decided to take her on publically, making many PR mistakes along the way. Hootie Johnson, the club president, refused to be 'intimidated at the point of a bayonet'. His comedy name and this fiery response replete with Civil War reference was the beginning of mass media coverage which, although serious, added greatly to the glee of the nation.

So, Martha took her protest south, giving the media what it wanted and taking the fight to the front door (well, the outer gates) of Augusta National. She'd received hundreds of death-threats so wore a bullet-proof vest. The implication was that these are red necks, or perhaps a sinister powerful elite, like something from a Dan Brown book, and that they'd protect their institution with guns. (To the plutocrats inside the gates the implication was that even feminists like to accessorise. Despite originally coming from Texas, she was a Yankee with a bee in her bonnet.)

But actually, changes were made, no doubt because of commercial pressures brought to bear following the NCWO's letter-writing campaign to club members, their companies and the tournament sponsors. Nobody would admit to such grubby considerations, but money talks and in 2012 women were allowed to join the club, starting with Darla Moore and Condoleezza Rice. Luckily Darla's a billionaire and Condoleezza makes up for the double-hit of being a black woman by also being a former secretary of state. Augusta housewives probably aren't holding their breaths.

So, people of colour and women are now welcome here. And the club, having got its house in order, feels free to carry on moralising. Tiger Woods' sexual standards are not in keeping with Augusta we were told by the club chairman. "It's not simply the degree of his conduct that is so egregious here," he said, as many reached for a dictionary. "It is the fact he disappointed all of us and more importantly our kids and grandkids," he explained, as even more reached for the sick-bag.

Despite all this rancour, the course's class is undeniable. Amen Corner, a three hole stretch on the back nine is worthy of worship. But don't call it the back nine. That suggests backside, which obviously suggests sex. (In fairness, I know golfers who would be in a partially aroused state if they got to tee it up on

11, 12 and 13.) So, television announcers are told to avoid this. They talk about the inward half or some-such.

Anyway, that's the way it is down Magnolia Lane. It's pretty stiff and hypocritical. But the crowds (the 'patrons') behave and there's much Southern civility and the downright decency of Bobby Jones still mostly prevails. They want to see how it rolls across town at a private aviation sponsored party, a fearsome entertainment on Magnolia Boulevard.

The women here are younger and lovelier than the men and a remarkable number of them, it's clear, aren't sporting underwear. I'm honestly not looking closely. No way: I might get caught doing that. And anyway, the guys are all Steven Siegal lookalikes, bulky jackets, loads of cash and slicked back hair. They might hurt me.

There's a practise putting green that's a dream to behold and I'm happily making my way round it, making friends. The drinks are extraordinarily good and I'm thirsty in the searing heat, parched thanks to the large Cuban cigar someone's given me. He's a businessman from North Carolina, a proper industrialist but a total riot. He introduces his best friend as his Samoan Attorney. This guy reads Hunter S Thompson for goodness sake! His wife's not Miss World, but she was Miss Winston and she's a riot too. Everybody's eating and drinking and smoking and putting and making merry. It's mid-afternoon, 90 in the shade. We have nothing to be unhappy about.

But it's that evening – Friday evening – when the jet party gets serious. Alcohol has truly been 'taken', as they say in Scotland ('do you take a drink?') and now it's time to dance and, well, as you do, take a quick golf lesson from Butch Harmon on the simulator. He tells me to 'compress it more'. He's right but I'm none the wiser.

A few big-name golf pros take the stage and take some questions. We all roar approval when one of them – still in the hunt halfway through the tournament so with a late tee time the next day – raises a large glass of bourbon. The real acclamation though comes when the boss of the jet company says a few words, all of them about his company's 100% safety record and the measures taken to keep things that way. I'd seen this guy around earlier and spoken to him and got a gruff word in reply. I thought he was like the bus driver who'd brought all the beautiful people here to party, that I might see him shuffling around in his tracksuit and sandals at the corner of the dance floor later, or maybe rolling a cigarette beside his coach at the end of the night. But no, he's the man! He explains there are countless thousands of safety checks diligently completed before each flight. And there are three or four pilots on each plane. Hey, even the stewardesses could take the controls in an emergency and they look great. We're all cheering our heads off like someone's made an overhead shot from the halfway line for a million bucks.

I've heard there are no bitter people in first class cabins. They think life's good because they've got more legroom and because the flight's shorter from the front. Tell you what, they'd be bitter if they could see it here. That's how the other half of the 1% live, they'd say, grudgingly.

I've never been on one of these things, these private planes. I don't know why I'm cheering. But we're all alive and these planes are never going down, never I tell you. We're going to live forever!

Next day it turns out we're not going to live forever. Who knew? The party's over, for us anyway. We're heading back to Atlanta, limping back slowly, stopping at every diner on the way, hungover and hungry. We're going to watch the weekend on television.

To be in Augusta when The Masters comes to town is wonderful. It's been a thrill. The golf world gathers and all Honky Tonk America lines up on Washington Road. The crowds are colossal. When they're inside the grounds they're patrons. But on the street they're a howling mob. Everything's for sale and they're throwing their cash around. John Daly's truck is parked up, selling who knows what, promoting anything anyone asks him to. He's got a big payroll. All his exes wear Rolexes, he sings.

Back in the big city we take it easy. It's mostly about recovery and televised golf but on the Sunday morning we head off to a course north of Atlanta, up in Ball Ground, so named because this is where the Cherokee used to play lacrosse before we chased them off the property. It's an amazing course with interesting elevation changes, nothing like the flat plains I'd imagined from the town's etymology. Built with Augusta in mind, the club is a private refuge for the privileged few.

It's maintained to within an inch of its life. To be precise, the grass is mown to within a millimetre of death. People forget this: cut the grass too low too often and it dies. But up here they know what they're doing.

The greens roll about the same speeds as at Augusta. Even the tees roll about the same speed as Augusta greens. There are holes cut into the tees on the par-3s so you can have a putt if you're waiting. But really, there's no waiting. There's nobody here.

But it's not perfect. Just as Augusta had Cliff Roberts, so this place has owners who do things their way. If they're out on the course, irrespective of your own speed of play, you let them through. It's not terrible. It's not a stuffy place. They just have this rule.

Anyway, I'm playing with my great friend Gene who 'hosted me' at The Masters, who's hosting me at his home in Atlanta, who hosts me at The Carnegie Club and Royal Dornoch in Scotland, who hosts me everywhere. (I think I once bought him a cup of coffee.) We're joined by his friend Chuck. Gene and Chuck can really play.

Gene's supposedly retired. He ran a successful engineering company and is now meant to be relaxing,
playing endless golf. But he can't help himself. He still
gets involved, businesswise, with things he's passion-
ate about. He's into country music and he's into golf
so can often be found in Nashville or in Scotland, the
clubs in the trunk, the radio blaring.

He funded his engineering degree at Georgia Tech
through part-time work in the pro shop at a local
club. And when he graduated he decided to give it a
go and joined the PGA. He stood on the range at his
first professional tournament and wondered what the
strange sounds were around him. Turns out they were
the acoustics of the very best shots, the near perfect
strikes which are the stock in trade of top golfers.
Gene reckoned there and then that he didn't have it
in him. Happily he turned out to be pretty good at
engineering.

On the course this morning Gene's pitching is off the
mark so he's taking short shots one-handed. He's an
engineer and if it's broken he fixes it. Southern boys
famously fix everything with duct tape and this is his
golfing equivalent. I've never seen him shoot worse
than two or three over par. Somehow he just finds a
way. Today he gets up and down single-handed every
time from within 30 yards. Meanwhile, Chuck birdies
all the par-3s. And, inspired, even I make a couple of
shots, minor miracles appropriate to Masters Sunday.

Back at the ranch, Gene's place, we have a huge family feast and gather in the den to watch events play out down the road. It's strange to be watching The Masters in daylight, strange to be watching it so nearby.

The talk is all golf and the local knowledge is for real. Chuck's played at Augusta often. A PGA member, originally from Florida, he's been out there on his own, the place to himself, waved on by a friend in the pro shop, unimaginable really. But that was the 80s. And Chuck's Chuck: well-connected, laid back, loveable. Everyone I meet who knows Chuck – which is pretty much everyone I meet – says something like, 'I'd walk over burning coals for Chuck' or 'any friend of Chuck's is a friend of mine' etc. And now I go around saying this stuff too. And now he's in a book.

Chuck's got the leathery sun-damaged skin you look for in a golf pro. If there were more movies about golf then casting directors would be all over him. (There are very few golf movies and they never really work because it's a game played inside the head.)

Anyway, were there more of these feature films, Chuck would get the part: Southern Golf Pro. You would never, never play this guy for money. That is, unless you've got money. And, because of the clubs he works out of and because of the sheer quality on show – his game, the advice, the look – there are a fair few high-rollers who take their lessons from him and probably play him for decent sums. He gives them shots. They can grease their irons (a bit of Vaseline on the face keeps the shots straighter). But I reckon very few ever win. Outside of golf he plays some serious poker and, Gene assures me, a mean game of gin. I've sat and watched them play cards for hours in their leisure gear. They get changed to play cards! But despite the sweat pants, it's not a spectator sport. It's golf you really want to watch them play: Gene with his outrageous short game and long drawing drives, Chuck with his metronomic, super smooth Southern swing.

Gene's played Augusta often too, done plenty of stints with friends in The Butler Cabin. No outsiders really know the secrets to accessing Augusta. And when someone learns the secrets they don't reveal them. But from general conversations I've gleaned that it goes something like this. First, you've got to be a trusted good guy and you need to know some members, senior members perhaps. Then you have to have the cash to make a significant charitable donation to the cause of that member's asking, many thousands for sure. And then – as a guest of that member - you pay for golf, your stay, the food, the serious wines cellared beneath the clubhouse. Clearly there are ways and means. But you have to know the way and you need to have the means.

7 TOURING, 3490

Beside my desk in the office is a waist-high pile of golf books, overspill from the shelves. At the top of them is a lovely hardback by James Finnegan: *Emerald Fairways and Foam-Flecked Seas – A Golfer's Pilgrimage to the Courses of Ireland*. It's a practical guide as well as a hymn to the glories of Irish golf.

Inside, in blue ink, in a joyful flowing script, is written: 'Augusta 1996, Loyal Goulding, Cork.' I guess my friend, Loyal, had been at Augusta to watch Faldo win The Masters. I watched it on television and it was painful viewing, the Englishman turning the screw while Greg Norman, The Great White Shark, turned to jelly. I turn to the edition notice, on the back of the title page, and I see this book was published in that same year. The printer's key reveals that it's a first edition.

I imagine a scene: beneath the giant oak in front of the Augusta Clubhouse, a group of Irishmen hold court. James Finnegan, the American writer, comes over to join them and gifts a select few a copy of his newly minted book. Back at The Augusta Country Club, where Loyal often stays when he attends The Masters, Loyal makes the book unique in blue pen. It's a beauty.

Loyal has been visiting Georgia during Masters Week since before it was in any way normal to do so. It started when he met Charlie Yates in Ireland and availed himself of a typically generous invitation from the long-time secretary of Augusta to come to the tournament. The two men quickly found common ground, starting with the great Irish golfer Cecil Ewing who Charlie had defeated at Troon in 1938 to win The Amateur Championship. Mutually they knew enough golf and golfers to sustain a lifetime of friendship and Charlie hosted the Gouldings at Augusta without interruption across four decades.

The brotherhood of Irish golf fans attending The Masters is considerable: Pat, Joe, Dermot, JP, Eoghan, Loyal, many others too, enjoying the golf and glamour and greenness of the occasion. Through the rest of the year, back home in Ireland, Loyal often wears his Augusta tie – Bobby Jones-style, just visible above his v-neck sweater – using it to get talking about his passion for the famous golf tournament and its Southern hospitality and, in this way, he would persuade others to join the throng.

I've come to know Loyal through my American friend

Gene who tells the story that he was into the first few days of the mother of all golfing trips around South West Ireland and was sleeping off some drinks in the sun when he met Loyal. (The Augusta tie got them talking.) They had mutual friends, including Mr Yates – whose acquaintance is a badge of honour amongst those who love the good manners and traditions of the game – and straight away Loyal was involved, helping with Gene's trip, calling his friends at various clubs to move back tee times so that they might better avail themselves of an extra Guinness (or so) each evening.

It was Gene who insisted I meet Loyal, saying he was the perfect starting point for the Irish golf education I was embarking on. Gene was financing a publishing project to create a beautiful collectible book, *18 Greatest Irish Golf Holes*, the companion piece to a Scottish edition he backed the year before. Gene told me that Loyal knows everyone and everyone knows Loyal. He wasn't wrong. Loyal was my entrée into the world of Irish golf. In the UK I might have carried a formal letter of introduction. But in Ireland, where things are more casual, more trusting, I just had to mention his name.

Behind me, on the wall in my office, is a map of Ireland and on it I've marked its golf courses, the 100 or so that I've visited. Even without turning around I can readily remember the places and names, stuff I'm not normally very good at. But in my head the map of Ireland is easy to see, maybe because like the mind palaces of great memory champions it's full of life, full of memorable names and characters, none of whom I've had to invent. Nor have I had to create clever mnemonics to remember them by. And better than that, for memory purposes, they're all joined up in my mind, because one would introduce another, one friend sharing their friends. I could add arrows to the map, plotting my trips around the island in the various directions I've been pointed in. "You must see Noel and he'll get you some salmon," or else, "visit Wilma and she'll tell you all about the new green on the second," or perhaps "meet Jim and he might get you out on a boat." Amongst the Irish one just needs a small connection and that's it, friends for life, and one friendship leads to another.

I drive off the ferry early in the morning and make briefly south to the classic links at Royal Dublin where Loyal greets me like an old friend, yet this our first meeting. We drive the course because Loyal, well into his 80s, will rarely walk a full championship course on foot. His knowledge is considerable. He has local knowledge everywhere we go. As well as the holes and their recent redesigns, he wants me to know about the ground we're on. "Have you seen Mutiny on the Bounty?" he asks. "Mel Gibson? Fletcher Christian?" as he mixes fact and fiction, perfectly knowingly. "Well, you're on a sand bank now. This golf course, the land it's on, Bull Island, it was made by Captain Bligh, Christian's nemesis. He had a wall built in the harbour to save the shipping lanes silt-ing up. And this is the result, the displaced silt, a golf course for the last 100-odd years!"

I've travelled through the night from southern England. But Loyal won't be letting up. We make for Portmarnock Golf Club, one of the many clubs at which Loyal maintains a membership, a great course on its very own peninsula. Arriving there is sensational, down an unsigned road that must surely, I think, be the wrong turning, but then the Portmarnock promontory is revealed, the red-roofed white-walled clubhouse seen from far off as you drive the small private track to the club's gate posts.

Players used to arrive by sea. Even when a road was introduced members still had to cross the estuary in horse and cart, water halfway up the wheels. The place was actually discovered on Christmas Eve in 1893 when a Scotsman and an Irishman in a rowing boat (this is not a joke) went looking for somewhere they might build a course. They were pretty pleased with what they found. That it was owned by John Jameson, a Scotsman who'd come to Dublin to make some money in the spirits business, was propitious.

"Now, you're going to meet Niall, who's my boy, my son. Now, he's in the bank but he's a very good golfer," explained Loyal. 'Very good' proves to be something of an understatement. These days he's an amateur with a full-time job and plenty going on as Portmarnock's Chairman of the Greens Committee. But once he was an Irish International and, eternally, he is the two-time winner of The West of Ireland, one of the country's most precious golf prizes. Niall, as solid and sound a character as his dad, does the course tour along with a golfing demonstration par excellence, sub-par perhaps.

"He was a great caddy back when he was a young boy," Loyal says, as if this might explain the golfing greatness I've just witnessed. "He would show me a couple of clubs, but the one he wanted me to play would always be held a little higher. And his selections were always good."

North of Portmarnock we speedily visit The Island Golf Club which, confusingly, is no longer strictly an island. In contrast to other seaside courses in this central eastern stretch, The Island has heaving dunes. Hole 13 is its preeminent par-3, the beach right and the grass swales left, the wind everywhere. The next hole, the 14th, was once the old first and is where early golfers would arrive by boat: shades of Portmarnock. My guide shows no signs of tiring on this long day and we head further north still to Baltray, leaving County Dublin and arriving at County Louth Golf Club, a fabulous and friendly club with a top-flight course in a very special corner of the country where the River Boyne meets the sea. Loyal, noticing my fatigue, offers me some respite: "Craig, we'll have a drink and something to eat, maybe some fish on the bone from Michael in the kitchen. We'll talk golf and we'll see the course in the morning."

I've never eaten better clubhouse food than that at Baltray, as County Louth Golf Club is mostly known. The wine's excellent. And, in the club's 12-bedroom hotel, I sleep the sleep of the dead, maybe because before dosing off I push on with the novel I'm reading, 'Shade,' by the famous Irish filmmaker, Neil Jordan, where the main character is, well, dead. It's set in Baltray, a Neil Jordan family holiday-spot, and it even makes use of the golf course. Unusually, the ending is revealed right at the beginning, so you know what's going to happen before it happens but you enjoy it nonetheless. Maybe I'm not selling it, but it's brilliant, keeping me awake longer than the long day should have allowed.

Loyal was very, very good at golf. It's cruel that age has diminished his game. But he doesn't seem to mind. He's happy on the course, straight talking about the game, about my game. He tells me to keep back, stay behind the ball, sway into it less, reminding me of the position Jack Nicklaus would set his head to before swinging. It's not much of an adjustment to make. In fact, I've made it before. But to be kind to an old guy I follow his advice closely and, inevitably, I start hitting thrilling shots. Loyal just knows golf. He'd seen an error and fixed it the simplest way. His one tip seemed to correct a myriad of faults. This one-time bank manager should have been a golf instructor. After a few holes of unusual excellence, he comes up with one more thing for me, "just one," he states, knowing no doubt how complexity can kill what ought to be a natural action. He reckons I can hit it harder. I do as he says. The advice is excellent. The stability afforded by staying back makes it suddenly possible to give it a decent whack. He says he saw it all clearly on the first shot I hit. It's funny because people will always tell me – struggling desperately to say something nice about my action – that I swing sweetly, that my timing's lovely. They might be right, but I also know they mean I could hit it much harder. In golf we learn that our virtues are often the same as our vices. But Loyal has given me a little platform from which to rectify a fault.

Baltray, with Loyal, is a high-point in the game for me: Loyal driving me around as he played every other hole, turning me briefly into a golfer and getting me back to the clubhouse in time for a typically tremendous Irish breakfast. "What did you think, Craig? Those par-3s are the best. Imaginative, aren't they?"

Loyal could talk golf constantly. It's joyful to play with this guy who knows so much and who doesn't want to keep it to himself. He talks golf and he asks me questions about golf, about my golf. I'd be happy to listen and learn from Loyal all day. His musical voice, now hoarse with age, is great to hear. But Loyal eventually sends me on my way, my education now commenced.

The resulting book, finished a year later, is dedicated to Loyal, something which he told me gave him much pleasure, even if it was tempered by some small displeasure at his beloved Cork Golf Club not featuring amongst its selection of the country's 18 finest holes! His affection for the work of Alister MacKenzie, above all at Augusta, Lahinch and Cork, knows no limits.

Over many months, back and forwards between England and Ireland, I visited Irish golf's holy places and met its holy men and women, my calling card or point of reference usually Loyal himself.

At Royal Portrush I have a particularly swift game with three octogenarians of Loyal's acquaintance, flying round the championship links, each of them carrying their own full-sets and each of them sporting various combinations of artificial hips and knees. They explained that because of grim experience during the Troubles, specifically gang punishments in the form of countless knee-cappings, their surgeons were the best in the business.

At Lough Erne, in County Fermanagh, Lynne McCool, the director of golf, takes me to a shebeen, brilliant and bonkers, all traditional music and Guinness and whiskey. That same night, very late, back at the hotel, we witness a corporate golf day perform old Irish songs, everyone doing their solo, singing in rounds, everyone listening in silence then calling out encouragement between the verses: "well done that man," or, "but Doyle can sing can he not?" Often the singer's eyes would be fixed firmly on the floor, singing unaccompanied, yet always with the most intense feeling. And I think, my God, what sort of country is this? These were the men who had that day been playing golf, who the day before had been supermarket managers or whatever. But that night they were artists with some sort of kindness and humanity which stretched back to their folk culture and their musical love.

I meet a lady at Ballybunion, a keen golfer, the captain's wife, who many years ago had worked for Loyal at a bank in Cork. She had wanted to take a Friday off work, ostensibly to go to her cousin's wedding. She wanted an advance on her pay as well. But Loyal is nobody's fool; he knew she was going to the Galway Races; still, he gave her the money and let her go to the important family day...

I'm in Tralee looking out at the course and the first people I meet are headed speedily from the 18th green to a private airfield. Their plane is taking them back to Boston. It's mid-Friday morning and they have a tee time booked later that day at Brookline. I tell them that I'm working on a book about Irish golf. Have I ever met Loyal Goulding, they wonder?

At Doonbeg I find myself playing golf, randomly, like you do, with a Brazilian shipping magnate, a beautiful and rich woman. I could easily have been lost for words, but we share friends and acquaintances. She's a regular visitor to Ireland. "Of course I know Loyal," she exclaims, and the conversation doesn't stop after that.

It was Loyal who made the introductions for me at the venerable Lahnich where I heard the happiest words uttered on a course. They were spoken by my host, Martin Barrett. It was a Saturday morning. The sun was shining, the dew burning off fast. It was 8am. We were a fourball about to play 7,000 yards of serious stuff. "Alright boys," he said. "We're going to be done with this links by 11am." I love golf, but I love it played quickly. Sure enough, we walk off the 18th green at 10.55am, having played at not more than a pleasant canter. A British Royal wedding is taking place that day. I'd hoped to miss it and I'm amazed that it's being shown on TV in a County Clare clubhouse. "The British were alright as enemies, you know," Martin says to me. "Other countries would have taken things worse." This had never occurred to me. Still, I don't stick around to watch the celebrations but take myself off to the shorter, simpler, Castle Course, the club's secondary links on the inland side of the Liscannor Road. Many of the holes are originals from Old Tom Morris's work. The 6th is no great shakes, technically, but it might be my favourite in Ireland. I could play it all day, this tiny par-3 in the shadow of the 15th century tower beside the estuary, the beach and the bridge.

Driving around Ireland is blissful. It's everything you could hope for. It really is green, the grass being actually greener. On its own out on the western fringes, Ireland has the longest grass growing season in Europe.

And the chat – the craic - really is good (and nobody ever says "top of the morning to you"). Back in the UK, radio phone-in shows are a minefield of mortification, people calling in who are ill-equipped to talk about anything. The opposite is true in Ireland, where everyone seems able to talk fairly well about anything, irrespective of knowledge.

And they understand golf. Irish newspapers on Mondays and Tuesdays give more space to it than found anywhere in the world. It's strange that Bernard Shaw thought that golf was 'typical capitalist lunacy of upper-class Edwardian England.' The great Irish dramatist failed miserably because it isn't upper class. It has the distinction of, mostly, being looked down on by the very posh. And in Ireland – as in Scotland and indeed in various distinct communities around the world – it is a game of the people.

The Irish are rightly proud of the courses they have. Their energy for the subject is part of their promotional skills. Ireland is one of the world's top tourist destinations: one of Ireland's great exports was its people and now their people's people return in a spirit of genealogical enquiry and golfing thirst. From Canada, Australia, New Zealand, but above all from The United States of America, they come to trace their ancestors, to examine parish records and stare at tombstones. But also, they come to walk the famous fairways. Ireland is effective in promoting itself as a great golfing destination because, firstly, it has the great fortune to enjoy fabulous natural golfing conditions, chiefly the sandy soils around its coasts on which its historic courses were built. But since then it has had the good sense to update those courses and build many new ones, especially through the 80s and 90s, boom times for the game here when the original links courses were modernised and lengthened and a slew of stylish inland courses were opened: in order of appearance Mount Juliet, The K Club, Adare Manor, Druid's Glen, Powerscourt, and even into the 2000s, Concra Wood, Lough Erne and Killeen Castle, to name just some. But none of this would have counted for anything if tourists didn't come back wanting more or didn't go home and tell their friends to visit. They do this because the Irish have natural charm. They look after their visitors and show them a good time. Irish hospitality is something to behold. It's not the efficient service and sometimes forced smile of some other hospitable places. It's a genuine interest and warmth and the ability to make time for you.

I call Loyal to update him on my progress. "Have you seen Ruddy yet?" he asks. "No? You need to see Ruddy, the sooner the better."

"Welcome," says Ruddy. "I've been following your progress. We've got mutual friends now you know. When a person comes to Ireland, they become a member of the family. Friendships are formed that last for decades. We notice a visitor and we embrace them. They are not just fodder to a business. They are very welcome. The world of Irish golf is close knit, but we're happy to let you in."

"How's the course?" I wonder, looking forward to seeing the linksland I've heard so much about.

"It's OK, thanks for asking. It'll be there for 400 years. But me, I'm going downhill fast."

I think he's joking. He seems in rude health, after all. "Don't worry about me. We're all going downhill, eventually."

"The course is great," he continues, "and getting better. You suffer to build a course. You work in winter. You might live in a hut: at least, I have. And like a painting it's a grey mess in the middle of the work. But then it can turn out bright, wonderful. It's like watching kids grow. You love them, then they annoy you and then they turn out grand. There's a rhythm in life like that, just like in golf. A course is like a kid: it's all about how it's reared. You know, the kid was fine when it was born but 16 years later it's in jail. Hopefully though we're rearing this one well."

Loyal Goulding, 1929 – 2018

8 HAPPY HUNTING, 1540

Ruddy tells me to "leave sex on the beach out of it because the only reason I ever went onto the beach was to find my golf ball."

Ruddy is the irrepressible intellectual Irishman who must feature at some length in all golf books worth their salt. He has been immortalised in print many times and when the final golfing hagiographies are written he'll be included in those too, no doubt in close proximity to the throne (on which will be sitting Old Tom Morris).

Ruddy loves books, so this might be gratifying to him. But we can be certain that what brings him more joy is that he is also immortalised in grass and sand at the many great golf courses across Ireland which bear his name: Pat Ruddy, architect.

He grew up out on the west coast, WB Yeats country.

The famous poet, famously, enjoyed his first romantic encounters on the beach there. It's in discussing this that Ruddy suggests I keep my dirty thoughts to myself. But he opens up about how childhood days at County Sligo Golf Club at Rosses Point were character-forming.

"To play the great links on the Rosses, day-in and day-out, was a privilege that could not be surpassed. To walk the same links watching championships in progress, or the great Cecil Ewing of Walker Cup fame in action every evening he was at home, gave an early clue as to how glorious this game can be when played properly.

"The Ewing swing was short. Very short. But the shots were long. Very long. The putting was deadly. Very deadly. He won over 20 championships and lost to Charlie Yates in the final of the British Amateur. A god amongst mortals.

"There were days when no adults would appear. Just a few kids would have a great championship links to themselves and the greenkeepers would kindly turn their eyes away and ignore the antics of youth. That great freedom is at the heart of The European Club."

It's an article of faith amongst visiting golfers to the country that South West Ireland is where it's at: Waterville, Tralee, Ballybunnion, Lahinch and a litany of other lovely links which roll off the tongue enjoy the lion's share of golf tourism. There's the 'northern loop' and there are the great courses of

Dublin Bay, some other natural geographic group-ings too. But Pat Ruddy, from a helicopter he'd hired, went about finding an alternative spot, seeking out little known linksland where he could build his own course. He found it south of Dublin at Brittas Bay. It's here he built The European Club. He built it and they come.

Links courses are, globally speaking, few and far be-tween so most golfers, inevitably, will never play links golf. Those who play it regularly are a rarity. Those who have a links course of their own are the select few. Pat Ruddy dreamed he might be amongst their number and by skill and luck and force of per-sonality the dream was realised. There was consider-able personal financial risk too. He didn't find himself a big-time international backer. He did it himself. He has an individuality which is brilliant and substan-tial.

Pat Ruddy is a journalist turned publicist turned pub-lisher turned tournament promoter turned architect turned course proprietor. His energy is endless and his design work all over Ireland is off-the-scale. But it is his own course, built on land lying idle for so long on the shore of the Irish Sea, which is his great-est achievement. It's one of Ireland's most celebrated courses, one of the finest in the world. Yet he and his family basically built it under their own steam and it's Pat or his son Gerry or daughter Sidon who will probably greet you when you arrive there. It's a fam-ily affair.

Ruddy is not the son of an architect, which is one way into the design game. Nor is he a former pro golfer, a big-name champion, which is another. Heck, he didn't even study it, formally. Rather, he's a golf fanatic who decided to live out his ideas, who decided to follow through on his dreams, the same dreams many golfers have in the clubhouse bar, doodling on a scorecard, while their pal is getting the drinks in.

His words have the cadences of poetry, I think. This is how he talks about the seaside game:

"Now, a links is the cream when it comes to golf. It is the original of the species and where the game began on sandy terrain along the sea. The dry going allows the game to be played in great comfort all year through and the combination of fast running ground, tall roughs and fine-grassed fairways and greens is quite intoxicating when taken together with the turbulent topographical heaves and the capricious nature of the winds that are, in turn, at their most baleful and most soothing where there is a conjunction of land, sea and air."

He occasionally likes to drive around the links at The European Club in his big old saloon car. Once, reversing up a fairway, he drove the car into a bunker. (Bad driving considering he designed the course...) Anyway, a visiting American fourball helped him out and he drove off, with a wicked smile, asking them to rake the sand. No doubt he fed them all apple pie and cream with lashings of tea when they finished their game. (The apple pie is serious stuff. Ruddy tested countless recipes before settling on the one now served at the club.)

"By keeping membership numbers low at all times," he explains, "and by controlling the number of visitors, the game is uncrowded for all at most times and, very important, the links is all but empty for prolonged periods when Ruddy can drive out to any part of the property, drop a bag of balls on the clipped grass and be back in Rosses Point in the 1950s once more..." (He often refers to himself by name, like a character in a story. And he often uses the personal pronoun, one. It's not that he's being grandiose. It's just that he is grand, in the Irish sense of the word: just grand, a grand character in a grand tale.)

"Rosses Point is in the northwest. The European Club is in the southeast. It may be at the other side of Ireland but it is on the same side of the moon which often appears before the last ball is picked up and one beats a retreat to the clubhouse to await another dawn and the same again."

His private collection of thousands of golf books are carefully stored in his library, upstairs in the family home which sits close to the course. Inside one favourite tome is a picture of Henry Cotton in action and beneath it the legend, 'The Irrepressible Thrill of the Downhill Drive.' Ruddy shows me this page proudly. He loves this. He feels it in his bones. The well struck shot is a sensory pleasure and he knows it.

Pat Ruddy could be some sort of medicine man, wise and witty, making you feel good. His courses make you feel good too, if you find fun in adversity. But if you're someone who likes a fictional account of their abilities, they may not suit you. They're tough, but if you can handle the truth about your golf his designs are perfect. They're carefully orchestrated, typically not too testing at the start, allowing some early scoring momentum, but there's always a challenge ahead. At The European that challenge arrives, most obviously, on the seventh hole, a long par-4, by common consent one of the world's greatest.

"That one is facing a giant task strikes home on the seventh tee," says Ruddy, with relish. "A seemingly endless stretch of gorse and grass, with a stream meandering across in front of the tee and close to the fairway all the way down the right to the green, presents a daunting sight. This is a 6-marker. (Golf holes can be categorised in the same way as examination questions: 2-markers, 4-markers and 6-markers which are compulsory and must be answered or a fail is incurred.) It demands a good straight drive and a good straight second. Hitting two straight shots in succession defeats most people and even the best find it a difficult task to perform at the same place over four consecutive days in a tournament.

"To set up the ideal approach one must drive straight down the line. There is room to bail out away from the stream to the left but this means playing back towards the stream with the second. You make your choices..."

Ruddy loves golf because it's whimsical, a sheer joy. But he loves it too because it's about primitive instincts found deep in our nature, our drive to overcome obstacles, to survive and thrive.

"The fairway on the 7th hole runs through a divine reed-rich marsh. There isn't a manmade thing in sight even as you turn 360-degrees mid-fairway. It's a magical place to taste the planet in its elemental state. To be down there golfing is to be a man with club in hand, out hunting!"

9 INTO THE AIR, 2890

Enthusiastic that all golfers might improve, the great teacher, at the age of 91, asks about my typical best and worst shots. I'm not holding a club. He's not looking at my swing. We're sat at his dining room table.

"My best shots are irons, hit with a little draw. The worst shots are my drives. I've got a two-way miss. I used to be able to drive quite well. But since getting older or since we started hitting it on the upswing, I'm never sure where it's going."

I answer questions about push-slice and pull-slice, stuff that must remain between pupil and master. He moves some coffee cups and water glasses by fine degrees, demonstrating essentials of swing path and clubface direction. Then the verdict is delivered. I need to strengthen my grip, just a jot.

"You've hit from the inside all your golfing life," he says, correctly. "And mostly you still do, but, especially with the long club, you're now often delivering the face open. The grip's a neutral one, which is good. Strengthen it a fraction."

The interview finished, and keen to take his advice, I head out of The New Forest, the ancient area of woodland and pastureland where the elderly sage spends his retirement years. I make for Remedy Oak, a nearby course he co-designed (a club with an excellent practise facility). It's member's only. But enlightened and confident, no questions are asked. The electric gates swing open. I hit 50 shots on the range, each one the best shot I've ever hit. They fly. They soar. And the hook spin is exactly as I want it to be. I've overcome gravity, seemingly defied science. Fear is gone. I'm guaranteed about, oh, one round of excellent golf before the magic wears off and I return to the old rubbish. Nonetheless, this must be why, for many years, many of the greatest golfers in the world, struggling with their swings, would all demand the same of their agents and managers. "Get me Jacobs," they'd say.

John Jacobs' driveway is packed with black German saloon cars. To my horror the great and the good of The European Tour are here, making a pilgrimage, paying homage, getting everything on tape. You see, without John, there'd probably be no European Tour. Certainly, he's the guy who jumpstarted it, who made it happen and in no small way made it what it is.

Somehow I've wangled an hour with him.

The rusting Honda is conspicuous amongst these gleaming machines, jammed into the last available spot. The worst thing that could happen now would be if the Tour's CEO should arrive in his limo. He does. I back my car out onto the little lane.

"I grew up in the north of England, at Lindrick Golf Club, a course on three county borders. Hit your second to the left of the fourth green and you're in Nottinghamshire, to the right and you're in Derbyshire, on the fairway or on the green and you're in Yorkshire. There's a little dell there where there used to be cockfighting. If the police arrived the organisers just crossed county borders.

"There's a Jacobs family plaque on the wall in the clubhouse. My father became the professional there after The Great War. He'd been badly gassed on The Somme and died when I was nine. My mother, who was a keen golfer as well, managed the clubhouse and we stayed on. She was wonderful. In the Second World War the golf club became a maternity home. A thousand babies were born there. My mum, Gertrude Jacobs, fed the nurses and the babies and the new mothers. She was a household name in Yorkshire for her cooking, Mrs Jacobs.

"I was maybe seven years old and I remember my dad cut me a tiny little wood and sent me off to practise. There used to be a ditch in front of the fairly high first tee. You can still see where it was. He told me to come and tell him when I could hit it over the ditch. And eventually I did. I still remember the feel of that club, the thin little shaft. I remember the ball flying over the ditch and I ran to him and I said Daddy, Daddy, I've done it.

"He was from Norfolk, one of three brothers born in Brancaster, on the north coast, The Wash. They were all golfers and the youngest brother, my dad, became apprentice at Royal West Norfolk Golf Club to Tom King, the professional who had once been apprentice to Old Tom Morris in St Andrews.

"We went back to Norfolk every summer. We stayed with my uncle and I played golf all the time. I used to play with Johnathan and David Cory-Wright, twins who lived there. Jonathan was killed in Germany in April 1945 when he was just 20. They were only five days younger than me.

"They were wonderful holidays and it's a superb golf course. You can't get to and from the clubhouse when there's a spring tide. The road from the village to the course floods and the course itself gets flooded and it becomes a links with ponds and lakes, an amazing thing. "But I'm a Yorkshireman and I should romanticise a little about Lindrick because I had such a wonderful childhood.

"There was a lovely gentleman there who was in The Royal Flying Corps in the Great War. He had a Tiger Moth and his wife had a Moth Minor, the one wing version. The aerodrome was only a couple of miles away. I was 13 maybe and they'd take me for flights in these beautiful old planes. Can you believe it? We'd fly over Yorkshire and the surrounding counties, over the course at Lindrick.

"Now when war broke out that gentleman got a winch launch where you pull rope across the aerodrome to get the gliders up and because of him we were the first Air Training Corps boys to learn to fly gliders and we all got our licenses pretty quick. I was straight into air crew. That was 1942. But I failed the medical, which probably saved my life.

"I had surgery and I recouped. I worked on a local farm, you know, the war effort. But I was waiting to go back in and when my time came they didn't want pilots anymore. They wanted flight engineers for the four engine bombers. So, I became a flight engineer on a Halifax bomber, an American one with rotary engines. I'd learned on the inline engines, the British ones, so I had to start all over again. But I got my wing and I was ever so proud. And then the war stopped the week after I was ready. How lucky can you be? Losses in Bomber Command were truly horrendous.

"I still played a bit of golf in the war. There was a ball shortage because the manufacturers were making munitions, probably. But the course was open. Well, there were old cars parked on the fairways, filled with stones. It was to stop the enemy landing. But I just played around them.

"Yes, I was lucky not to fly in the war, although I was

disappointed. My friend Laddie Lucas was Douglas Badder's brother-in-law and his biographer too. Laddie wasn't the name he was christened with. The men of a highland regiment used to call after his nursemaid, 'how's the wee laddie?' The name stuck. But anyway, I taught Douglas to play golf. He was very good, but came a cropper when he turned too far or gripped too tightly. He had strong arms though. He played to six or even lower eventually."

Wing Commander Laddie Lucas was a distinguished RAF officer, the son of a founder of Prince's Golf Club in Sandwich, Kent, leading amateur in The Open in 1935 and, for a time, probably the finest left-handed golfer in the world. He captained the 1947 and 1949 Walker Cup teams. He was a Member of Parliament. He wrote a sports column for The Sunday Express. And he wrote countless books, mostly about golf and golfers, flying and airmen, including a biography of John Jacobs. A plaque at Prince's Golf Club shows where he made an emergency landing in his Spitfire after it was hit over the continent and only just limped home. His local knowledge saved him.

Sir Douglas Bader was a fighter ace with 20 aerial victories to his credit, this despite losing both legs in a crash 10 years before war broke out. He is forever famous for his flying brilliance but also for the endless escape attempts following his capture in 1941 when he bailed out over occupied France. He was immortalised in the film Reach for the Sky, in which Kenneth More plays the great man. When he was knighted it was for his tireless work for the disabled community.

So, this is how it was for John: his great golf ability and his great teaching ability saw him move in rarefied circles.

"But growing up I played with the Artisans and my mother was in the Ladies Artisans. In those days only the wealthy played really, especially at weekends when they played two rounds each day, which was easy for them because they had caddies, you see. But we Artisans played at certain hours, up early in the summer for a fast game and then you could play after four o'clock. But High Days and holidays we'd have to rake the bunkers or fill divots or what-have-you.

"When Laddie and I started the driving ranges donkeys years ago we did it to get people started on the game cheaply. It's still too expensive. It takes a long time now to play and there are probably too many clubs in the bag. It's a better game with fewer clubs because you have to make up more shots. Nine clubs would raise the standard and let the best players shine through. Yes, nine clubs and nine or maybe 12 holes.

"We had a few businesses along with the golf schools. I made some anti-slice clubs and I thought I was going to get rich because in America in their first year they sold like hotcakes. They weren't offset so much as just more upright and they worked. We had them at the golf schools for people to try and someone who'd been pushing shots like billyo would try one and hit it dead straight but we didn't know how to sell them here and they didn't make them as well over here. And then they wanted them for the guy who hooks all the time, but that's just 20% of the market. Anyway, it was giving lessons that I loved.

"My first job, out of the services, was assistant at Hallamshire, close to Lindrick. The secretary explained I'd get two pounds a week from Mr Wallace the professional and 30 shillings from the club. Golf lessons were five shillings an hour so I'd get two and Mr Wallace three. After 6pm I'd keep the whole five shillings.

"OK, what day of the week do I get off? But there was no day a week off. There was no day in the year off. To get there on Christmas morning I had to catch the milk train from Shire Oak station then walk across the fields and get the train to Sheffield and then a taxi so I could work all day washing up in the kitchens for the 30 or 40 members who were lunching in the clubhouse.

"I didn't really know how to teach but I was learning on the job. I was enthusiastic at least because they all came back for more. Rita and I got married on that little early success, teaching late in the long summer evenings and making that little bit more money.

"I remember one of the first lessons I ever gave was to a dear old boy with hickory shafted clubs, a terrible golfer, shanked everything, so far over he got everything in the heel. There was nowhere to teach so I gave lessons on the right-hand side of the first fairway and he was shanking everything over the wall. How the hell can I sort this guy, I was thinking? Well, I moved him closer and closer to the wall and he smashed a club on it. I thought crikey maybe I've taken this a bit far. But he said give me another club and he smashed it as well and I think it was the first time he realised what he was doing wrong. And so I had to sell him an entire new set of clubs.

"Anyway, it was a good experience because this guy with the shank learned for himself. But like I say I must have been enthusiastic because my lesson book was soon choc-a-bloc just like it would be later in life.

"But I still played competitively when I could. It was only really in Cairo, my next job, that I wasn't competing. It was the biggest clubhouse outside America with horseracing, cricket, tennis. A huge thing. Then in 1952 the place went mad and we had to hide. I was teaching one of the King' equerries and he got a big fire engine to take us into a government office in the city to get an exit visa. I remember hiding in the back of it in the middle of Cairo surrounded by a mass of screaming people, the revolution raging around us. Never been so frightened in my life. If the door had been thrown open I don't doubt we'd have been torn to pieces.

"We got the visa and some South Africans I'd been teaching found us a driver who was sworn to get us portside for a boat at the Suez Canal. Eventually we were on a lighter underneath this huge ship which would get us out of there and we were very relieved indeed. Rita and I were just married and we got a cabin together and, well, it was the best journey ever.

"Of course, back home I was desperate to play golf again. All players were club pros really. It was a different life then. The second triumvirate, Hogan, Nelson and Snead, they were all club pros.

"I was on the third tee morning and afternoon when Hogan was on the sixth tee at Carnoustie. We played 36 holes on the last day of The Open, you see. So I saw what he did there. Let's paint a picture..."

John carefully manoeuvres the crockery so that Hogan's Alley opens up between the coffee cups and the plate of chocolate biscuits. Water glasses and jug are commandeered as well.

"There's the tee. There's the green. There's the out of bounds. There's the flipping great bunkers. We all hit it to the bunkers and maybe slid it off to the right because there's more fairway there. But Hogan just ripped it out there low and straight for the out of bounds, fading it back in, round the back of the bunkers. The books of course don't convey the speed of the swing. Like lightning it was."

For Hogan, famously, the truth was in the dirt, as if it's what we do on earth that counts, which is a grand way to say you can learn a lot from divots. John Jacobs doesn't disagree with this. But he prefers to see the ball in flight, sometimes – and this was his trick - even observing the ball but not the swing and giving advice accordingly, deducing the process from the outcome, Sherlock Holmes-style.

"But Byron was my favourite, an opinion slightly coloured by meeting them both and Byron becoming a great, great friend. I won my matches in the 1955 Ryder Cup at Thunderbird Country Club you see because I'd been there the year before when Byron got two or three of us Brits out there for the first Thunderbird Invitational. I really liked that course and I finished in the top-10.

"But my teaching reputation was increasing, which I didn't want at first, because I wanted to be playing. Yet I've always thanked god for a gift, the teaching one. It's a wonderful wonderful thing because you're dealing with people the whole time, making friends, passing on expertise which is fulfilling, even if I once did tell a Belgian princess she was the biggest hooker on the continent, but she knew what I meant.

"When I was a child the professional would stand and look at you, not at the ball. That's the blind spot for me. I'd look down the line where you can see the swing path and the golf ball and, quite clearly, the position of the clubface. A golf lesson for me is diagnosis. What is this person doing right or wrong? Then there's an explanation which must be impossible to not understand, simple correction. And I turned out to be pretty good at it. I didn't think I was being revolutionary. I just knew it was the easiest way to do it. The flight is commensurate with the skill employed delivering club to ball. The shot, its shape, its speed and time in the air describe the swing."

John Jacobs, 1925 - 2017

10 NATURAL REBIRTH, 3110

Adult resignation replaced youthful hopefulness for Tiger Woods. His trajectory, once so dizzyingly stratospheric, became far less thrilling. This is not simply the natural way of things, a long upwards curve and a slow steady decline, the naturally diminishing effects of age. His has been a mesmerising rollercoaster. Had his golfing attainment graph simply followed nature all would be well, golf being the game for life, the fifth and sixth decades still being good for the occasional victory. But his career fell over the cliff.

It happens to us all, the change from young and hopeful to older and somewhat resigned. Between those two points are the moments that make us, the moments that make up our lives. For Tiger, between those points was a golf-career that was second to none (ok, second to one perhaps). Tiger set the golfing world on fire and then suddenly, shockingly, was no longer the force he once was.

Woods' greatness was blown away in a sudden storm. Over time some of the pieces were found and returned to him. But it doesn't all - quite - fit together. Often he's been unable to golf because he's injured or because he's trying too hard or else because he looks like he doesn't mean it and is playing without intent. In the worst years, when Tiger Woods was on the tee, driver in hand, people didn't want to watch. The two-way miss, like the yips, is catching. And then he was shanking his short chips. Look away please people. Nothing to see here.

Tiger is not the golfer he was, even when standing back in the winner's enclosure. We all carry pride and hurt in various measure and those things impact us. Tiger always carried a lot of pride, and with good reason. Some felt he had too much pride, that he was arrogant. But of course he was proud and inevitably there was an arrogance. For a long time he was the best we'd ever seen. For years the difficulties inherent in golf, physical and mental, seemed not to apply to him. Those who were critical were looking for too much in an athlete. Part of his brilliance was intimidation and aloofness. It worked. He almost certainly wasn't the world's greatest bloke. But he was certainly the world's greatest golfer. Maybe you didn't like it. Maybe some observers didn't like that he tore up courses, tore up the form book, reinvented the game, or that he was young and black and brilliant and rich.

To go back to the beginning, there was a little kid out in California who could play some golf. Age two he made his debut on national TV, appearing on the Mike Douglas show, on the same bill as Jimmy Stewart and Bob Hope, who he had a putting contest with after first hitting a few delightful drives. He was so cute, so charming, with his little golf bag and long flowing swing and steady head. Of course, his dad, Earl, was there on the stage with him. Earl was the one who drove Tiger to great things, pushed him on, persuading him of his golfing destiny, making it come true.

Tiger grew up golfing at the Navy Course in Orange County, playing with dad and his old military buddies. Dad, a retired Green Beret, had access to the course beside the Joint Forces Training Base at Los Alamitos and this is really where it all began when Lt Colonel Earl Woods introduced his young son to the game. Age three, the kid would shoot 48 over nine holes. The scores kept getting lower and the young prodigy would become a fixture here for many years.

He often played at Heartwell Golf Course too, down at Long Beach. This little golf course has its own monumental place in the annals of the game. On August 27, 1980, age just five, Tiger Woods made his first ever birdie here on the third hole, just 91 yards long. Heartwell is an 18 hole par-3 course.

Age eight he could break 80 and he would win The Junior World Golf Championships: he went on to win it five more times.

Age 12 he could break 70. The kid could play and his father had an ambition in mind for him: to be the best ever, to win more major championships than Jack Nicklaus. It's a big ask. I guess there are mums and dads who might want their offspring to be doctors or maybe just hope they'll be happy and kind. And then you've got Earl Woods who sees some remarkable achievement, something that most people say will never be done again, and he wants his boy to better it.

Lovely little Eldrick Tont Woods - who would become Tiger (a nom de guerre, the nickname his father gave him) - was growing up into a big, handsome, slightly goofy looking guy. Still, beauty smiled on him whenever he picked up a club. As a child Woods suffered with a speech impediment, a stutter which he overcame with professional help and 'hard work and a competitive spirit,' precisely the stuff he used to dominate his sport. He communicated very clearly with club in hand. I am the best, he said.

He was the youngest winner of the US Junior Amateur, a tournament he would win three times. He became the youngest winner of the US Amateur and then, the next year, 1995, he enrolled at Stanford. Of course, he could have gone to any college, but Stanford had been making a play for him forever and its significant academic reputation appealed to him.

At Stanford he lived out the last of his ordinary life, as ordinary as it can be for a college sports star. He roomed with his great mate, Notah Begay III (not someone from the pornographic film business, despite the name); and he worked hard and he golfed hard.

He found time to win the US Amateur again in 1995 and 1996, the first person to win three in a row. He was the best unpaid player in the country, by a million miles really, and he decided it was time to get on tour. So, in a decision which made sense at the time but which 20 years later he'd say he regretted, Tiger became the world's most famous college drop-out, leaving Stanford after his sophomore year in which he won eight tournaments, having won three in his freshman season.

Why did he come to regret the decision? The allure of the cash mountain waiting for him must have been considerable at the time, but later in life, in retrospect, with so much money securely banked, it probably seemed like something he could have put off for the sake of spending a little longer as, roughly speaking, a civilian and not as the world's most famous sportsman.

Tiger signed a $40 million deal with Nike, a five-year arrangement in which the professionally unproven golfer would wear their apparel and, eventually, play their equipment. He was 19. Of course, he delivered for Nike and Nike delivered for him. His successes on the course were extraordinary. He won a couple of times in that first short season of his, amazing really.

And the next year, 1997, Nick Faldo helped him into a green jacket. Tiger had become the youngest winner at Augusta, the first black winner. He hadn't three-putted once. Most of his putts were uphill because he was hitting wedges into the greens. The course had never seen the likes. He had finished 12 shots clear of the field, his 18-under par score being a record until 2015. And that's despite taking 40 shots on his first nine holes. 40 shots... Really, that's poor scoring, despite the southern breeze whipping through the pines. But then, suddenly, he went ballistic. He came home in 30. Friday he made 65, Saturday 66. Shooting 69 on the Sunday, television golf audience records were broken, a legend was born, new fans were created and golf exploded back into life.

I knew a Spanish exchange student that year. He didn't have much English, but we communicated in the language of sports and I no doubt demonstrated my fondness for golf with a swing. 'Ah Tiger Boots!' he said. And for the rest of his stay he'd always say the same thing when he saw me. And even now I often think of Tiger Boots, not Woods, but Boots, the amazing breakthrough superstar even non-golfing continental Europeans knew about.

Much debate about golf's decline should look back to the '97 Masters. Up until Masters Sunday that year, golf was simply golf. After that it became golf in the Tiger Woods era, which is an entirely different beast. Perhaps the real base measure for the sport should be somewhere before this point. What came for a few years afterwards was unnaturally inflated by the glories and glamour of one man and by his almighty propaganda machine, Nike, churning out clever content around its star athlete. That participation numbers and course builds went through the roof only to drop back a decade or so later should perhaps be removed from all industry equations. Woods was an unfathomable exception and, surely, not to be repeated.

Nike came up with a $100 million contract extension in 2001. It was extended again in 2006, for seven years, for a sum so sizeable I can't quite confirm it, presumably so large nobody could write it down.

In 2013 it was announced that the relationship would continue, this despite the fall from grace that had happened in the meantime. But the sponsor realised that while Tiger was still gold, he could no longer be the golden boy. He had become something different, some sort of necessary legacy piece. His golf was faltering and his image was hit and a new high-profile stable mate was required. Enter Rory McIlroy ($155 million on a 10-year contract) and cue a lot of commercials featuring the young gun jokily taunting the old stager, as boring and predictable as they sound.

Tiger, Rory and other top-end golfers played the clubs with the swoosh on them, drivers and irons developed at vast expense and promoted endlessly. But somehow their efforts didn't get through to the public. They never sold that well: I still don't know an amateur who plays those clubs. And so, in 2016, the big brand announced that its club making days were over. Colossal sums had been spent. Major championships had been won but the net return had been less than zero and the enterprise was withdrawing from the golf hardware business.

Tiger wasn't responsible for this commercial failure, exactly. Other forces were at work, not least the traditional conservatism of the golfing majority who reckoned the brand was too athletic, too basketball, too street. But no doubt Tiger's downfall was expensively unhelpful. At the end of 2009 the world learned that he was less than faithful in marital terms. The media interest was colossal. Waitresses and adult actors and nightclub managers were thrown into the spotlight because of their various liaisons with him. The moral majority were quick to jump ship. Blue-chip sponsors dumped him fast. Shareholder losses at these companies amounted to more than $10 billion, a report established. But Nike stuck with their man. Maybe they could turn it all to their advantage with candid advertising and moody, staged expressions of remorse.

Meanwhile, pro golfers globally were trashing their burners, not their old TaylorMade woods but their secret mobile phones... Golf and golfers were in the spotlight.

Tiger's dad, who died in 2006, had been a massive philanderer. He paid for his pleasure, literally. And

paid again, because it was a long cause of friction between father and son. So, it was ironic – and predict-
able – that a father's vices might show up again in a
son's behaviour, especially when the dad had been the
man to give so much direction in every other respect.

The shame and pain Tiger felt were palpable. But his
apologies always felt insincere because they were so
heavily stage-managed as to appear absurd. Tiger's
advertising – through his sporting sponsor - was always excellent, if you like that sort of thing, but his
PR was always appallingly handled, insincere hog-
wash.

More than family breakdown, pain and shame, there
was a loss of prestige. It was almost like a confidence
trick was exposed, the curtain pulled back and the
legend caught with his pants down. Look, he's just
like us, we all thought, but he's worse. He's at it with
everyone! Tiger had become unclawed.

He was a person of consequence and then became a
person of ridicule. The haters and the moralists did
that, but he did it himself too. He diminished himself,
deliberately in some way. The most intriguing aspect
seemed to be the porn stars and the threesomes. But
much of it was prosaic stuff, sad and strange in suburban Florida.

The year before the scandal came out he had two knee
operations. He's had many more since and none has
been wholly successful. He's had back injuries and it's
been operated on too. These have all been very real,

but it's worth noting how emotional an injury to the back can be. A weakness was found inside him and he couldn't help but find more of them.

Sometimes it feels like he's on track again: his family life becomes as normal as divorced domesticity can be; he finds himself dating nice girls whose fathers clearly didn't get the memo to lock up their daughters; things are good; he wins tournaments; he's on the up again; but something regularly gives, be it muscular, skeletal or psychological.

No doubt he's moved on from his indiscretions. But perhaps we, his audience, haven't moved on. Tiger, because he's played golf all his life, knows that no matter how sanctimonious and self-righteous the wider world, we play our shot, good or bad, and we move on. It's always all about the next shot. The bad shots need to be forgotten. Even the good shots are wasted if the next shot is poor.

Golf's a game in which we keep our head down and keep going at least until we get to the 19th and grab a drink and sit back. Only then should we look at the scoreboard. But Tiger, it was felt, stole an early look at the scoreboard and concluded that he wasn't going to add too many more titles. We golfers all believe that the game holds thousands of lessons for us, all of them pointing us in the direction of a good life. Yet the game's greatest exponent, it appears, hadn't absorbed so many of these.

But coming out of the long, cruel slump, he has embraced an opportunity, towards the end of a career, for some sort of renewal. The great golfer is noticeably more human and says the right things about the importance of family and friends so that we actually believe him. He wins at Augusta National and it's hard to remember him asleep behind the wheel, up to his eyeballs in prescription meds.

If I was Tiger's friend or agent (kind of pathetic that even now I'm still having these little reveries) I would try to give him back himself. I would try to give him a love for the game and a fresh desire – not the old desire – to be amongst the best.

The demise of his famous sponsor could have been the moment to grasp back some of himself, using it as a moment to bail on the deal altogether, taking off that cap and giving up the swoosh. He could do as every neutral's favourite European football team did and sport the logo of a universally-admired charity instead of a corporate entity. He could carry his own clubs in a small Sunday bag. He could give any winnings to excellent causes. Like a pilgrim, with no possessions, he'd walk the fairways, unbranded. Like Samson, his hair (metaphorically only) might regrow. People would stare, but it would be wonderful. Maybe this is all too much like some strange mortification of the flesh, but it's got to be better than that stupid confession he did with his mum in the front row.

He could at least give up weight-lifting and start yoga.

He could spend some months in Machrihanish or Islay or some far flung Scottish golfing outpost and rediscover himself, connecting with people personally.

At Waterville House on the west coast of Ireland I've communed with the young Tiger Woods, staying in the room he slept in when there on a pre-Open warm-up tour round Ireland's linksland, getting into the groove of firm fairways and blustery winds in the company of older and wiser, though less brilliant, golfers: the steady Mark O'Meara and the ebullient Payne Stewart. Woods was at his best back then. An out-of-season extended trip back to County Kerry might be just the thing, a little fishing, some golf, some Guinness, some craic.

He still, often, looks like a man with seemingly unbearable quantities of pain, and nobody likes to see that. What people like to see is a great comeback.

We imagine the young Tiger had immediate, immoderate success with the golf swing. In fact, he worked long and hard, driven by his father. He knows how to put in the effort. But now he should put effort into making this comeback gentler, less intense, and even more successful. The heavy-lifting has been done. Now it's time for a lighter approach, a fun take on things. He needs to hit the dance floor and turn back time. He's swayed around for too long to the tune of his dad and his agent and his corporate partners. He got bored, got burned and took his eye off the ball.

Golf is optimistic, the most optimistic of games.

Some might think it's depressing, a slog when playing poorly, which is why Tiger ended up on his sofa playing video games and popping pills. It wasn't because his dad was dead or because he'd been inadvertently cruel to his little family. It was because his game was gone. But there is always a glimmer of hope, the next shot and the next. Opportunity knocks for the man who tees it up. Throughout his 40s and 50s he will find a way back. He's too good not to. His famous target, the Nicklaus major record that was pinned to his bedroom wall, can be met and overhauled.

Everything that's gone before: just eschew it. Good things are coming: just do it.

11 SOLSTICE, 1640

T he short night is coming to an end. The sun will soon rise into a clear sky. The possibilities are endless. Someone could do something serious with the coming day, something good, something great. Or they might choose to play golf...

Time spent on this game is significant. Equal time spent on languages or an MBA or somesuch and we'd all be accomplished or rich! But golf, for many adherents, requires none of the ambition or discipline that learning foreign tongues or acquiring wealth does. You may need to take a deep breath and make a strong coffee to sit down in front of a Mandarin textbook or draw up a profit and loss document. But with golf, well, you leap joyfully into your 1990 Japanese saloon, point the silver bonnet west towards the seaside, and you set off. At least that's what I'm doing today.

I'm thinking about all that time spent, the hundreds of rounds, the balls hit, the mental space given to the game, the courses replayed in my head just to kill time... I should be more useful at it by now, but I lack some natural ability and despite everything just said I actually lack playing time. Years have passed without a single shot being struck (though all the time I was entertaining the same golf dreams and visions). But what I've really lacked is resolve.

Were it the Chinese language lessons or the business qualifications I'd have a clear aim. But my golf has been without focus. It's been a pleasure but it's had no real purpose. Maybe a day like today can justify it.

This is a special day, Midsummer, my mother's birthday! And here in South West England – the home of Druids, Neolithic monuments and appropriated Arthurian legends – it's a big deal.

I'm driving past Glastonbury Tor, the hill which rises surprisingly out of the flat flooded lands around it. The sun's not up but the sky is light. The Tor can be glimpsed across much of the county, but this view, from a ridge to the south, is more pleasing than many. Today it's apparently floating, larger than usual: a Fata Morgana, morning mists or maybe my bleary eyes.

Midsummer, to state the obvious, comes just once a year. If all goes well you might get 80 of them. But subtract the ones you didn't notice. Forget the ones at the beginning and end. Consider just those you were aware of, the ones you gave some thought to, and it's an exclusive run. Doing something specific will celebrate the day and forever frame it. I'm setting out to do something I'll remember.

I'm headed to Burnham and Berrow Golf Club, the home of Somerset's best course and, for many, Somerset's second-best course. I'm destined for that second-best course which suits me fine. It's called The Channel Course. Elsewhere many nine hole add-ons are the 'wee course' or 'relief course' or 'family course'. But this is the real thing, a bona fide beautiful links, and a day ticket here is one of golf's great bargains, especially if you're going to do as I am and play all day. I'm going to play with direction. I'm going to enjoy it. But to make it meaningful, and perhaps to make it bearable, I'm going to set about it with intent.

I've switched off my phone (though I'll switch it on at some stage to call my mum). I've told almost nobody what I'm doing. It's to be a real experience, just for the sake of it. The only thing that could ruin it would be if I were to shoehorn it into a book sometime…

The notion of this long day of golf began to form itself back as a student member at Royal Aberdeen in North East Scotland. Displayed in the clubhouse there are the scorecards from Harry B Lumsden's nine rounds played on one day, June 27, 1908. He started at 5.15am and finished at 8.30pm. He averaged 82.2 shots per round and is reckoned to have walked 35 miles. What did he have for breakfast?

Today won't be the first time I've given up a day to golf. Iain, Stuart, Boydy and I would often play 36 or more holes in the summer holidays at Greenock. And I'd probably have played a couple of holes to get from home to the clubhouse to meet them and I'd play the first three again to get back at night, two short par-4s and a little par-3 in the dark. A little bit later in life, with university friends, Neil and I, sometimes with Richie, or once or twice with Louisa and Fiona, would manage 36 at Blairgowrie during the summer holidays.

Dedicating a whole day to leisure, an almost un-imaginable adult indulgence, is commonplace when you're young. As a grown up I had to start writing golf books in order to do anything similar. Long days spent alone golfing in East Lothian or County Kerry will never be forgotten and never repeated. I would sometimes walk two courses and play two courses: better than having a job...

I've got an ambitious target in mind today: to play as many holes of golf in a day as the best professionals play in a typical four-day tournament. Ancient people once conveyed giant stones improb-able distances across this landscape from the Welsh Mountains to the plains of Wiltshire just because it was important to them. Mr Lumsden played 162 holes of serious championship golf. Surely I can man-age 72 fairly short holes.

15 minutes into my first round I realise I've taken a gimme and played a mulligan. I'm not cheating (they all say that), just playing casually, unconsciously,

which is often fine, but not today. There'll be no more picking up on the green. Not holing out is strange, like not finishing a sentence, starting out to make a point but not quite managing it. And there's to be no free reloading on the tee. It's bad practise to be dishonest with oneself, though sometimes the deception's preferable to the truth: 46 shots for the first nine holes, 11 over par.

The second round is better: 42 shots, 7 over par. Throughout it I'm thinking hard about where I'm going wrong, trying to find something. On the ninth – having so far strengthened my grip and got nothing, having better braced my right knee and got nothing, having lifted my chin and got nothing – I think about keeping my head steadier, eliminating any sway. I stretch my shoulders a little bit before I swing. I keep still and strike out and hit the shot of the day. I've remembered the first lesson of golf, to keep one's head steady. How could a golfer of 28 years' experience forget such a thing?

The long day has dawned. Others are on the course. The clubhouse is open. I pay my green fee and grab a coffee.

My only ambition today is to play eight rounds of nine holes, honestly, mindfully, maybe to improve or at least to learn where I need to improve. But there's another hope: that I might shoot par for one of the nines. My third attempt is very close, just a couple off target. It was the eighth hole which ruined the scorecard, a short par-3. It's smaller than another hole of that number, The Postage Stamp at Troon, and it's harder to hold. It's disobedient. But that's a compliment to a golf hole. I made five on it.

My fourth round is one better, just 36 shots, many good, some excellent. It's the eighth hole again which defeats me, but I know I'll get another chance shortly. This is the speeded-up version of golf's one great, redeeming constant: there's always another day. Here, in about 90 minutes' time, a bit more having had something to eat, I can try again.

Fred Hawtree laid out this course in the 70s. Later, his son did some work here, altering fairway lines and building this eighth hole. I might write to him about it. Dear Martin, it's my favourite hole but too tricky. With golf there's always an architect or a committee or an ice age to blame for the lie of the land.

Now begins the fifth round. The scoring doesn't improve. It gets worse. Perhaps I should have stopped for lunch sooner. There'll be no par golf today. But my game remains reasonable. To play golf well is to be inside oneself. And to be inside oneself is, partially, interesting.

The final three loops are played with a half-set. But if my game's increasingly off it's not because I ever find myself between clubs. It's because I'm tiring, aching even. It would be easier to establish the meaninglessness of golf, rather than its meaning.

Time pierces me with some sadness. It's late. I should get home. My children will be in bed. My wife will be mystified at best. Much work waits undone. I'm getting older. But maybe I've learned something. Certainly, I've had fun and made something of my time on the coast by the Bristol Channel. Just as a slave setting foot on a British naval vessel becomes a freeman, so the golfer is liberated when he steps onto the links. And despite the conditions and aims set for the day, perhaps because of them, I've enjoyed my freedom.

Late in the evening, the sun below the horizon, light fading, there's only one way this is going. The sky is blue and black: nautical twilight. Time's a thief. The eighth green evades me again. The darkness steals my ball on the ninth, my 72nd.

A sigh of weariness. The dimity - which is what they call the evening afterglow in these parts – gives way to night and I head happily to the Honda.

12 IN OFFICE, 3040

He loves to golf, does the 45th President of The United States of America, just like many who came before him.

It's reckoned President Taft was the first First Golfer. His predecessor, Teddy Roosevelt, may have played the game too, but it was Taft who first came out, who first openly played it, who first extolled it.

"You know my tendency to golf," he once wrote, "my sympathy with anybody who wants to play it, and my desire to spread a love for the game whenever I can. Golf is a splendid recreation which can be enjoyed with profit by the young and the old. It is in the interest of good health and good manners. It promotes self-restraint, and, as one of its devotees has well said, affords a chance to play the man and act the gentleman. It is the game of all classes, not a mere plaything for faddists, nor, as many suppose, a game for the rich man only."

And with those words he teed it up for countless other commanders-in-chief to walk the fairways.

Woodrow Wilson, who followed him into The White House, was very keen but less than useful. His scores were high despite a dedication to the sport that saw him notch up an estimated 1200 rounds while in office. After him, Harding played, almost equally enthusiastically. In fact, Warren G had Harding Park in San Francisco named after him. Next up, Calvin Coolidge golfed. Then there was Herbert Hoover: not a golfer. But FDR was useful before he contracted polio. As a student he won the club championship at Campobello Island Golf Club beside his family's summer home in New Brunswick up in Canada. As President he brought in the great public works projects which included Bethpage Park in New York, home to some of the nation's finest municipal courses. And there's a course in his name in Philly too.

Truman didn't play. But then came Eisenhower who was famously into golf. He had the putting green built at The White House, was a member at Augusta and, when back in Washington, played regularly on another Alister Mackenzie course at The Burning Tree Club in Bethesda, Maryland.

JFK – one of the most skillful Presidential golfers - played at 'The Tree' too. So did LBJ, Nixon and Ford. Carter wasn't a golfer. But Reagan and then George H.W. Bush played, often at Burning Tree. But that club didn't do it for more recent Presidents, presumably because it aggressively excludes women and the world has, mostly, changed.

Clinton golfed. George W as well, but in troubled times he learned to stay off the course as his critics found it convenient ammunition against him. Post 9/11, fighting in Afghanistan and Iraq, it just didn't look good on him.

Next up, Barack Obama: the first person of colour to hold the great office and – let's hope historians remember this too - the first Presidential golfer to play left-handed (not the first left-handed President). Barry played a lot. But he was cautious to begin with. He didn't play once during his first 100 days and, even as he got into the swing of things he rarely took advantage of the great courses available to him, choosing instead, mostly, the military set-ups at Fort Belvoir and at Andrews Air Force base where the cost to the tax-payer was lower and the accusations of prestige and privilege couldn't be so easily levelled against him. As a candidate, Barry played basketball. As President, he became a dedicated golfer, playing 306 rounds in eight years in office. But conservatives were unforgiving. It has been permissable for most US leaders through the 20th and 21st centuries to play golf, but they turned on Barry big-time, a jumped-up negro costing us money was the subtext to their complaints.

Then came Donald Trump, the second person of colour (spray-tan orange, admittedly) to put his feet up on the Resolute desk in the Oval Office. Trump, despite his advanced age and girth, is maybe the best of all Presidential golfers. A member at Winged Foot and owner of 18 wonderful clubs, not a decent set of forged irons and a few spare hybrids, but actual clubs, with courses and members and guests and hotels.

For The Donald there is no difference between desiring and doing. He just gets on. We can all learn from him and golfers especially can learn a lot from him. Visualise the shot and hit it. Often it comes off. Picture your dreams and realise them, no matter how outrageous (and, in Trump's case, ostentatious).

Unlike his predecessor, President Trump quickly threw himself into the role of First Golfer, playing six times during his first month in office. (Your average golf writer doesn't hit the course nearly as much.) Back when he was just a self-employed real estate developer with a sideline in reality television perhaps golf outings were racked with guilt, but now with a steady job he can get out there on the course again, not a care in the world.

He has a funny old putting stroke yet is useful on the greens. His swing is idiosyncratic too, sweeping and swerving around his immense backside and waist. But Tiger Woods has been impressed at "how far he hits the ball at 70 years old," adding, "he takes a pretty good lash."

And yet his hands are small, the subject of much meanness but here the subject of a serious point: almost all the really good golfers I've met have big hands. Yet Trump – who raised his little paws aloft at a rally and announced he can hit a golf ball 285 with them – gets away with it. So, he is a man who can overcome shortcomings. Despite those diminutive digits he is clearly a man of excellent timing, some strength, some skill and supreme confidence, the ideal candidate to lead the free world.

Or not? Golf, we know, reveals much about a man. It undresses him, reveals his true character. We hear this constantly because there's much truth in it.

In the P.G. Wodehouse short story, *Ordeal by Golf*, Alexander Paterson visits the narrator, The Oldest Member, to ask his advice about appointing a new treasurer at the Paterson Dyeing and Refining Company. The Oldest Member, a comedic sage whose name is never revealed, dispenses some sound thinking, worth quoting in full:

"The only way of finding out a man's true character is to play golf with him. In no other walk of life does the cloven hoof so quickly display itself. I employed a lawyer for years, until one day I saw him kick his ball out of a heel-mark. I removed my business from his charge the next morning. He has not yet run off with any trust funds, but there is a nasty gleam in his eye, and I am convinced that it is only a question of time. Golf, my dear fellow, is the infallible test. The man who can go into a patch of rough alone, with the knowledge that only God is watching him, and play his ball where it lies, is the man who will serve you faithfully and well. The man who can smile bravely when his putt is diverted by one of those beastly wormcasts is pure gold right through. But the man who is hasty, unbalanced and violent on the links will display the same qualities in the wider field of every-day life. You don't want an unbalanced treasurer, do you?"

We don't know that America's leader is hasty, unbalanced or violent on the links. We hear, however, from many sources, that he is not exactly a man to play it as it lies and is likely to lie as he plays. That God's watching him when he's alone in a patch of rough matters not to him, we might conclude.

Samuel L Jackson claims Trump cheats. Oscar de la Hoya claims Trump cheats. Alice Cooper claims Trump cheats. Several prominent media commentators say the same. That's actors, boxers, rock stars and journalists. The next terms in the sequence are buy-to-let investors, serial killers and priests: the full rogue's gallery of golf partners lining up to make accusations.

Newspapers, naturally, have run their own investigations into Donald's rumoured dishonesty on the course. They've found lots of smoke and plenty of fire. Mostly though, here's what they've found: if a man flies you to a golf course and his name's on the plane and his name's on the sign above the clubhouse and if it's an excellent layout and he's fun to be with and the golf's gratis and lunch is paid for and if he miraculously finds his ball in the bushes who's complaining? Sure, the media has some good solid sources, but it's dismissed speedily: fake news, Donald says.

Even just toiling on the fringes of the golf media I find myself sharing mutual acquaintances with the 45th President, none of them willing to be named here and all of them anxious to point out that despite various failings he's entertaining to be with (like anyone might be if he had a skyscraper of his own). But there's no getting away from it, many who have golfed with the leader have noted a discrepancy between shots played and shots recorded.

The wise golf writer, David Owen, reckons, having golfed with Trump, that he is good, maybe as good as he says he is, but that he has a cavalier attitude to counting. Some time on from a casual game of friendly gimmes and various gentle liberties Trump phoned him up questioning why the article he'd written about their round together didn't include Donald's score, a 71, no mean feat at Trump Bedminster but not a number the journalist remembered being achieved in any accurate manner. But he gives the President the benefit of the doubt, reckoning that in Trump's mind he is not cheating or lying. Writing about that game in The New Yorker he says: "In Trump's own mind, I suspect, he really did shoot 71 that day, if not (by now) 69." To paraphrase another one of Trump's accusers, it's not that Trump likes to cheat but that he likes to win.

If we think competition is the defining characteristic of mankind, and especially if we think winning is our goal, then golf is not for us. Golf is competitive, sure. We compete against others and, unlike in many other pursuits, we compete against ourselves. Yet in golf the winning is not everything. It's already been said a zillion times: in golf we lose; we hit imperfect shots more readily than perfect shots; nature triumphs; the elements defy us; we handicap ourselves so we can play more fairly with our friends; and decencies are applied to this game more than to many others so that most golfers will never jump in the air to celebrate a victory before they've spoken with and shaken hands with their opponents.

Yet Trump, we feel, doesn't enter into much of this. He's obsessed with winning. Apparently he picks the best partner on the first tee. He's not shy of a long gimme or the mulligans which Bill Clinton made famous. He shouts down those who claim otherwise. He's won an improbable, a probably impossible, 18 club championships – he says - though investigations reveal various miscalculations there. As with his politics, facts and dates are often ignored and he presents slogans, symbols and sensation.

And this is a serious and unsafe approach. When it's all about winning, people are only interested in what they can do, not what they are. If Trump must always, in his mind, emerge victorious, he'll learn little about himself or the people he governs. In fact, he'll find he has little interest in the people he governs, everyone apart from him being a loser.

Still, it's got to be a good thing that he golfs. The devil makes work for idle little hands and golf is doing something, something meaningful this book seems to be arguing, something somewhat removed from the grown-up world of duty, from the presidential world of pressure. It's a game in which, if one can just be honest, successes are tempered by failures. We experience glory and insignificance in equal share when we play. And, experience being better than knowledge, this turns out to be a great lesson. It shows us the self, successful and otherwise. We learn that what goes up must come down. I guess I'm saying that even if some of this is lost on the 45th President, it's got to be good for all of us that the man plays golf. On a subconscious level, some of golf's lessons must surely be getting through to him.

But it seems that much of golf's appeal for Trump is in its prestige. He's a showy, casinos and boxing and beauty pageants kind of guy and he sees golf as part of that, something to do with economic privilege. He also seems to understand that it's a sport which, in parts, enjoys some social advantage and he's anxious to get a piece of the action there as well.

Although born to massive riches, and although he has power beyond dreams, Trump is still - strange as it might seem - an arriviste with his glorious working class Jersey accent, his brash brilliance, his exceptional but underdeveloped intellect and his dangerously narrow world view. Despite all he's achieved he'll always be an outsider, a man on the make.

He owns one of the classic Open Championship venues, yet it seems suddenly not to be on the tournament's rota, and that's despite its glorious history and amazing redesign in recent times. It is the most brilliant of Open courses, modern and thrilling, old and lovely.

Trump knows how good it is. Apparently even the rigours of the presidency don't stop him communicating regularly with the R&A about the changes made there, constantly politicking them to make sure the ancient championship is again staged on its fairways so that he might one day hand over the Claret Jug on the 18th green, indeed might even see his name engraved on it in the form of the venue, Trump Turnberry.

Building or buying great courses looks like just another way into the establishment for Trump. What he doesn't realise – and really he's lucky not to know this crap – is that golf's not top-table stuff. The British upper classes (I know, whatever...) refer to golf as sergeant's polo, and from their lofty heights that's not a compliment. These posh non-golfers sneer at us, imagining that the game is run by ex-military types of a certain bearing, all blue blazers and soup-stained trousers. For some on Wall Street and for much of The

City of London, golf is déclassé.

Many intellectuals and writers look down on the game too, fancying baseball or boxing or soccer, or so it sometimes seems. Poor golf, it turns out – who knew? - is actually a victim of snobbery. Of course, it's also riddled with its own snobberies.

Golf certainly fancies itself as having a high-brow literary canon, but much of it, the earlier stuff certainly and a lot of the British material, is the warbling of the privileged few, paeans to the amateur game and those who could afford to turn down professional pay checks, to competitions between grand universities or minority schools, celebrations of what might keep people out of the game and not what might get them into it. It's the sort of stuffiness one finds at some of the game's traditional haunts: Augusta National, Muirfield, The Royal & Ancient, The Tree... Trump, no matter how many billions he earns, or how many terms he serves, will never impress these people.

All lives, even Trump's, must be incidental, fleeting. That said, I'm sure he's making plans to live forever. And if that fails I hear he's funding nanotechnology research so that he can pass through the eye of the needle and go to heaven. Maybe then, golfing for all-time, he'll learn that the Scottish Judeo-Christian game is not one of power and prestige and patrician self-importance and whatever distortions have attached themselves to it over the years. Rather, it's a game of endless, eternal, struggles, where humility brings success. Therefore, it's a good one for Presidents to practise.

He isn't, any time soon, going to become a world-weary existentialist, but I'd like one day to hear that he had golfed on a rough and ready nine-holer somewhere random, had played with a couple of locals in light rain without an umbrella, had played badly, lost and loved it. But it's never gonna happen.

I'm at Trump Doonbeg in County Clare, Ireland, on the Atlantic coast. Last time I was here it was just plain old Doonbeg, no prefix. Now the prefix is everywhere and there's a lot of gilt about the place. There's a massive bowl of golden golf balls on display.

Last time I was here was with my friend, Justin. I was golfing. He was surfing. The weather was phenomenal. We'd go our separate ways early, staying out all day, meeting up late afternoon, wind-swept and with tales to tell. But Justin won't be back, not since Trump bought the place. It's not political idealism exactly. I mean, Justin works for a hedge fund. Rather, it's about getting to the beach.

At Trump Doonbeg, as well as at Trump National Golf Club Los Angeles on the Pacific coast, there are public rights of way – access paths to the beaches – across the courses. They're kind of charming, not uncommon at coastal courses, a happy reminder that, here, you are most likely on holiday. Stylish golf magazines always have a picture of a surfer strolling across the fairway at a seaside course. It's an incongruous image that makes sense. Golfers and surfers are into the elements. They're different ball games and surfing's tough and dangerous and golf, well, golf's golf. But we all like being out there doing our bit in nature. Anyway, apparently, Trump hates these access paths, cannot stand them. Trump doesn't want to see a man in neoprene anywhere near his links, thanks very much.

13 DOWN WITH
WOOD, 3880

Elegant and empirical, Panmure's clubhouse is something to behold. Apparently, it's based on Royal Calcutta Golf Club and celebrates the jute trade which long linked The River Tay, here in Scotland, and The Hooghly River in Bengal, India.

It was at Panmure Golf Club, a lovely links beside Carnoustie, in Tayside, on Scotland's east coast - around the bay from St Andrews really - that Ben Hogan practised in 1953 when he came to play the links game for the first and only time. He learned to use the small British ball here, learned how to sweep it off the firm sandy surfaces. Playing the course constantly for two weeks, just Ben and his caddie, Cecil Timms, he then went to Carnoustie and wiped the floor with all-comers in the national open. And he's still well-remembered here at Panmure, not least in the sixth hole which bears his name.

This week Panmure has been hosting its own open tournament, won, by 10 shots, by Sandy Lyle. The tournament, which is the most coveted in a burgeoning retro golf scene, was played over two rounds. With wooden-shafted clubs, Lyle shot an astonishing opening three-under-par 67, followed by a 71.

115 players from 20 countries competed for the World Hickory Open, amongst them the very best golfers with the wooden shaft, 15 of them professionals, many of them low handicap amateurs. At the prize-giving, to rapturous applause, Lyle was introduced as a four-time major champion, having won The British Open in 1985, The US Masters in 1988, as well as The World Hickory Open in 2014 and again in 2016.

It's what you might call a convivial tournament. Many of the competitors are friends to begin with, certainly friends by the end of a week which includes a team event and international triangular match, all played out on nearby classic Scottish links courses. There are no outsiders here because everyone is made welcome. Hickory golfers, it seems, are one big happy family and they're open to incomers. Chinese industrialists mingle with Swedish golf aficionados, Japanese doctors, US entrepreneurs and German aesthetes. In its camaraderie and low-level eccentricity it's a little like The St Moritz Tobogganing Club, all tweed and speed, because most players dress traditionally and none play slow.

Looking at the fashions on display you might think of the Steampunk phenomenon, the Victorian styling minus the industrial sci-fi. Or you might be reminded of The Goodwood Revival, a popular motor sport festival which takes place in the south of England where thousands of visitors dress in period clothes. But there's no official dress code at The World Hickory Open. It's just that almost all go to some effort and it feels like flat caps, especially the large newsboy-type berets, might almost be compulsory. Certainly, there are no baseball-style hats on show. The women are in long-flowing skirts. The men, mostly, are in plus fours, knickerbockers or knickers as the visiting Americans call them (which confuses the Brits who imagine knickers to be slightly saucy underwear). On the range an Italian player tells me that wearing plus fours and long socks is incredibly empowering, and sure enough, he hits some shots Payne Stewart would settle for. There are a lot of ties and v-neck pullovers. And nobody seems concerned that a tweed jacket might restrict their backswing.

Paulo Quirici, a Swiss professional, formerly of The European Tour but more recently a hickory champion on both sides of the Atlantic, sports a just-above-the-knee cream raincoat when he tees off on the first day in a passing rain shower. His swing - which like many here, is full and flowing - isn't constrained by his dapper accessorising. He loves the sport and loves the fashions too. In just six years playing with hickories, Quirici has become one of the traditional game's most prominent advocates, even persuading regular tour stalwarts Miguel Angel Jiménez, Lee Westwood and Danny Willett to join him in a much publicised fourball hickory exhibition at The European Masters in Crans-Montana.

When Lyle first won The World Hickory Open in 2014 he wasn't fully adorned for the occasion. This time though he's been sporting plus-fours which he says were a struggle to get over his large calves. Even at 58 he's a muscular man and still hits a mighty ball. With his first shot of the tournament, admittedly wind-assisted, he drives the ball through the first green, some 300 yards away. His playing partner, Rymer Smith, from West London, takes a 2-iron and holds the green, leaving the ball just 8 feet from the hole. Rymer, a scratch golfer, with an adjusted hickory handicap of 3, is the son of Joe Smith, author of the fascinating *Gypsy Joe: Bare-Knuckle Fighter and Professional Golfer*. Joe's a connoisseur and collector of hickory clubs, a very hard yet very gentle guy. When he was a boy he had a hickory club amongst his first set and he's been in thrall to them – and their inherent difficulty – ever since. This week though the course beats him up. Still, Rymer did him proud. Just 21 years old, he won the Archie Baird trophy, the prize for the top amateur, with a gross score for two rounds of 150. And his little brother Joe jr, (barely out of short trousers and now back into them in the form of Donegal tweed plus fours) collected one of the children's prizes.

The talk in the clubhouse might sometimes be of Fair

Isle sweaters and knitwear for the discerning gentleman. But mostly it turns to clubs. In fact, deals are going down all around. Money doesn't necessarily change hands in the car park. That would be impolite. But gorgeous old collectible clubs are shown around, much desired and occasionally bought and sold.

Sandy Lyle won the tournament with replica clubs, made for him by Tad Moore, the celebrated US designer who now turns his hand to new hickory-shafted clubs. Similar modern matched sets are available from two other prominent producers: Louisville Golf, whose owner, Mike Just, sadly died a week before the tournament and for whom prayers were said and glasses raised; and The St Andrews Golf Company, Scotland's last-standing golf club manufacturer. Clubs from these companies are authentic period replicas, very beautiful in their own right. But for some, not least the Swedish contingent (20 Swedes played the World Hickory in 2016), they are not sufficiently authentic. On the Swedish hickory scene only pre-1935 originals are allowed. It's a romantic rule, a wonderful notion, but reality bites and while hickory golf grows in popularity the supply of pre-1935 clubs must always, obviously, remain fixed. Worse than that, as demand grows supply decreases because hickory golfers, once they've swallowed the kool-aid, find themselves buying more clubs than they could ever play with. Most become collectors (as well as, by necessity, repairers and restorers). Soon, there simply won't be enough clubs to go around. And price inflation is considerable. Many hickory golfers would as soon part with their Tom Stewart niblick as a serious musician would with his Antonio Stradivari viola.

It's understandable. Each and every hickory club is unique; each has its own playing characteristics, varying flex and torque. And the golfers are constantly seeking the ideal instrument, the perfect mashie or mid-iron for their purpose. Then another comes along, a little lovelier, and it must be theirs. Yet, it's still hard to part with the others. The British Golf Collector's Society, well-represented at the tournament, is full of grown men who, in the presence of a collection of antique clubs, become like Harry Potter in Ollivander's wand shop, excitably seeking the perfect implement, the brassie or baffy which will allow them to work their own brand of magic on the course.

So, hickory golf has its problems. But, everyone at the tournament agrees, it also contains solutions to some of the issues facing the modern game of golf.

Tackled using hickory clubs, the older courses, ones now considered too short, are brought back into play. (Distances achieved with hickories are 10 or 20% less than with contemporary equipment. Most players use soft, modern golf balls, but you can subtract another 10% for those uncompromising few who use replica early 20th century balls.)

Playing shorter courses means playing faster rounds, a good thing in our time-pressed days. In fact, irrespective of the length of course, hickory golf is definitely played faster. That might be explained by the attitude and expertise of the players. But more than that it's because it's a game of feeling. Sure, with smaller sweet spots it's also a game of increased precision. Yet that only seems to speed things up. Imperfect strikes are inevitable. Nobody is careless, but the players push on and play in the moment. Perhaps expectations are slightly lower and, in fact, more realistic. ('Golf's not a game of perfect,' someone once wrote, wisely, but with no respect for language!) There's little backspin available with these clubs. So, alignment partially gives way to invention and imagination. Somehow it takes less time to thread a running shot between bunkers than to measure the carry distance over them.

The clubs are more delicate than today's modern weaponry, but they're pleasingly sturdy and light to carry. Nobody takes carts. Everybody walks: not many of the hickory golfers here are BMI-challenged. And there are claims to better health and fewer biomechanical concerns. Playing with hickories is less tiring, they say, the clubs benefiting from a slightly less aggressive swing. And, they add, the back doesn't hurt as it does with 'steels'. With 'steels' you aim and really go for it but with the wooden shafts you must be more creative, the torque affording more chance to shape the shots.

The hickory game certainly takes us back to whatever it was people first found enthralling in it, the essence of golf perhaps. Sandy Lyle sees it like that.

"It's great fun," he says. "Golf simply cannot be mastered. You have it for a while. Then it leaves you and hopefully you get it back. Hickory golf is harder still to master and that's what makes it a joy. Tiger has expressed an interest in it, you know. We were talking about it at the Champions Dinner at Augusta. I've actually sent him some clubs. I don't know how he's got on with them yet."

Hickory clubs typically don't have numbers. They have names: brassies, niblicks, baffing spoons, playclubs, mashies, mid-irons and many more. And while the champion may have pocketed some small change, the overall feeling is that hickory golf is definitely not a game of numbers, but of fun and fraternity.

At the heart of this fraternity is Lionel Freedman, the Championship Chairman who founded the event back in 2005 at Musselburgh when 36 players took part in the World Hickory Open (which that year could have lived without the grand global appellation as most of the participants were from Scotland's capital, just a few miles along the road).

Lionel, in his younger years, was a serious golfer. "I played a bit," he admits, before describing a glorious defeat at the hands of Henry Cotton. (Lionel, a nervous wreck he claims, played in a Pro Am match with Henry, but acquitted himself well, in no small part thanks to the telegram sent by friends on the morning of the game, delivered to his room at Gleneagles, saying simply, 'Make Cotton Reel'). There was another glorious defeat to Bobby Locke, a mere three and two. "But I was a businessman for my sins, a stockbroker once, an entrepreneur thereafter. Golf was something else, my raison d'être perhaps!"

Lionel was a West Londoner, born in Chiswick in 1934. But he would become a Berkshire and Surrey borders man by dint of his passion for the game, golfing regularly at Coombe Hill, then residing for many years on the Wentworth Estate, by the 15th hole of the West Course, part of the coterie of successful stockbrokers and celebrities who enjoyed their leisure in these parts.

Times changed for Lionel and in 1995 he moved to Scotland. Retired, divorced, living alone in rural Perthshire, he was golfing mostly at Comrie and St Fillans.

"It was a strange time but a good time too," says Lionel. "They are the most charming courses, Comrie and St Fillans. 18-holers are the heart of the game, but sometimes nine holes, played quickly on a quiet course in beautiful surroundings like those, have a vitality the bigger number can't match. They have a concentrated significance that's special. They suited me very well then."

Comrie's high on the slopes of the north side of the Earn Valley, a heathland challenge with spectacular views. Some miles further down the glen, almost on the banks of Loch Earn itself, St Fillans is less hilly and no less lovely, a parkland gem. Geographically, this is the centre of Scotland, and Lionel was in love and decided to stay. In 1998 he remarried, moving to East Lothian, just outside Edinburgh, because his new wife, Beth, was a Musselburgh lass. Lionel became Secretary and Treasurer of Musselburgh Old Course. Musselburgh was once the centre of the golfing world, home to many great professionals and centre of the ball and club manufacturing industry. The course here was one of the original Open venues. But at just nine-holes laid-out inside the race course which was created around it in 1816, the professional game of golf was always destined to outgrow it. When Lionel joined the club it was languishing somewhat, despite its distinguished past. But he revived the old links, overseeing various improvements, not least to the club's finances. It was a labour of love. He adored its unique place in the game: it was at Musselburgh that Mary Queen of Scots played in the 16th century; it was where, in 1829, a tool to cut the regulation 4 1/2 inch hole was introduced; it's also where the sole plate was first fitted to wooden clubs, 'brassies', protecting them from the hard-paved roads that run along close to the first few holes.

In 1999 Musselburgh hosted an outing of the British Golf Collector's Society and Lionel witnessed, for the first time, hickory golf. He was struck by the joy shared by a happy few and was soon golfing with similarly ancient sticks and sharing in the fun. With the zeal of the convert he became involved across the wider world of hickory and six years later was staging the inaugural World Hickory Open which, annually, has grown more and more successful and played no small part in the increased popularity of the form.

"Less is more, in terms of the clubs we carry," he explained to me. "With the full 14 you spend time wondering which club to use. With a few less clubs in the bag the time is spent, more interestingly I think, wondering how to use them. It's not that there's less precision. There may be more precision. In fact, the possible combinations of shots and clubs are numerous. But feelings and instincts quickly overtake complex calculations and these are generally more fun than mathematics and data."

That word 'fun' keeps coming up.

"There's a little less certainty with hickory clubs. And if you're not a control freak, there's fun in that. You see, the modern game lets technology rule the roost. Older courses are humiliated under the onslaught of the newest clubs and balls, massive drives and biting back-spin. So, we need bigger courses and we need more time. These are two things that for us humans are currently finite. Nobody's building more land. Nobody's finding us any more time. Therefore we should look to these older courses where the challenge, with the original clubs, is as interesting as ever. The contours of the land are fascinating. Intelligence, tactics and close thought are required. With the older clubs on the older courses the game is played on the ground as well as in the air and touch and feel are more important than brute force. If I had to explain it all in one word I'd opt for fun."

But Lionel has never been stuck in the past. Even in his 80s Lionel makes excellent use of his various social media streams and conducts his hickory affairs across many time zones with video conference calling. The 2017 World Hickory Open was sponsored by a California-based networking organisation, LinkedGolfers.

"We're into networking and we're into golf and hickory golf's numbers are good and growing and even though it's a small percentage of my network that plays the hickory game, they're amongst the most social," says Sean Kelly, the company founder, who doesn't do the Zuckerberg grey t-shirts but goes for quite a bit of tartan and plus-fours, at least when he's on World Hickory business. He plays with replica classic golf balls too, the sure sign of a purist (where many are happy to use modern, low-compression ammunition).

"Although I love my new life in Scotland," says Lionel, "I sometimes think, if I was a younger man, I'd consider heading to California. A lot of the future comes out of there, it seems. And there's a good hickory scene going on. There are quite a few Californians here this week," he points out.

"Yes, I appreciate the past, certain standards, values and structure and all the things an old man like me might be expected to admire! But in golf terms what

I see in the past is an answer to present problems. And I think these problems should be taken seriously. I truly believe golf represents a good avenue to happiness and wellbeing. Other sports do too of course. I love football and I still follow Arsenal, always have, through thick and thin, thin and thin actually is how it sometimes feels to me. But there's more to golf than football, maybe because it can be played at all ages and taking part is generally more rewarding than spectating.

"The happiness and wellbeing in golf lasts a lifetime. Its pleasure is immediate but also deeply retrospective. Look at all the stories we've already shared about various games and courses, in my case some of them 60 years ago! You play a game of golf and you think about it afterwards. To an extent you analyse it and hold on to it and hopefully learn from it.

"It's why I firmly believe hickory golf should be played with replica clubs as well as the originals. If we don't allow that then we can't grow the game and I really believe our hickory game has relevance. We become irrelevant if we only allow originals. It limits us. It prevents take-up. It becomes expensive. Maybe the replica clubs do have some small advantage, though I'd calculate it at no more than a single shot in a round. So there should be different sections within tournaments, pre-1935 clubs and more modern varieties. It needn't change anything. There would still be overall winners and various flights within a competition for different equipment. It may be something we introduce in The World Hickory Open. I trust golf has a long and important future ahead of it and I really hope hickory can be part of that, a big part of it even."

Lionel always loved working and always loved playing. He reckoned though that one complimented the other, that leisure is only leisure when it is in contrast to work.

"It's always been great to golf, but it's especially great to golf when it's a treat, a change from the day-to-day in the office. I suppose I'm from that generation that was a little less hands-on at home - the men I mean - and maybe we could go golfing in a way that's not so easy now when domestic life is shared out more equally.

"In my retirement years, you see, I missed work so I made golf my work, both Musselburgh Links and Craigielaw Golf Club in Aberlady where I became captain and then of course The World Hickory Open too. I love throwing myself into The World Hickory. The next few years are mapped out, great golf courses, the best in the world even. There are some wonderful tournaments ahead for us and much organising to be done. I just know it's going to keep on growing and getting better. But we have to put in the work."

I tell Lionel about how, in the future, work might be harder to find thanks to artificial intelligence, cyborg job-stealers. I imagine I might blow his mind but of course it turns out he knows all about this stuff, probably from all his long Skype calls with California. He thinks, as I do, that people might fill their times – usefully – with golf.

"A lot of clubs have artisan sections, members who earn playing privileges through course maintenance. There we have the work-life balance, perfectly encapsulated, a bit of golf and a bit of greenkeeping. And if the golf played is hickory golf then everyone can learn how to repair and maintain, even create from scratch, their own clubs. You can't take any pleasure from looking after a modern driver. All you can do is wipe it down with a cloth! But the satisfaction to be taken from looking after wooden clubs is something.

"I really think there's a full and happy life to be had in golf. I've had one. There are no regrets, though it might have been nice to have a few more years with the hickories. I came to it a bit late. And I've not played so much recently. I've not got the terrible back and knees of some lifelong golfers. What I have is old age!

"Using hickories has been good for the joints. The sets are smaller and the bags are smaller. You can't thrash out at the ball with these clubs. It doesn't work that way. Of course, strength is still something. Look at Rymer and Sandy and the way they hit it. But ask them and they'll tell you they're swinging more carefully with hickories because they have to. Their expert timing is the thing more than their strength. With hickories, the swing becomes slower and more deliberate because to really hit out at it is to fail. The wooden shaft will not quite catch up so less effort is required. Less is more with the hickory swing, something of a simplification but partially true. The point though is that it leaves some energy for the important things, the camaraderie, the relationships."

Alex Bruce is a Scotsman, a St Andrean no less, who now lives in Japan where, with his Japanese friends, he is part of the informal 'Happy Hickory Golfers Society.' A number of these happy people have travelled from Japan to take part in the tournament.

"The whole point is to be happy. It must be the thinking behind golf," he says, "otherwise what is its point? Certainly, it's the point of hickory golf. But you only realise that fully when you play it, ignoring the bad shots and celebrating the good. It's just a niche aspect of the game right now. But maybe that's why it brings so much magic to the people who take part."

Lionel Freedman, 1934 - 2017

14 EAST OF EDINBURGH, 5230

I'm late, driving from the Highlands down to East Lothian where, in Gullane, The Hawg awaits. He puts some stock in timeliness. He knows I'm a slacker but I'd like him to think otherwise, so I drive fast. I'd said I'd be with him in time for dinner. The Hawg, I speculate, typically dines late. But, then again, he's Scottish and practical so it could be early. The road's clear. I think of my dad's warnings about the A9: Scotland's most dangerous road; better late in this life than early in the next etc. I remember the lessons from a 'defensive driving' course my father and I took back in the 90s, staying away from other cars, second-guessing their moves, making my own intentions clear. But I still put my foot down. The Honda, the silver-bullet, responds, slowly...

The Hawg's rented a house for a week. He's running on the beach every morning, taking on much protein, playing 36 holes every day. His girlfriend and various pals are coming out from Edinburgh throughout the week to join him. I'm a guest for two nights. The steaks – it's sure to be steak, serious cuts – will be coming up to room temperature on the kitchen table. The wine – it'll be red and French and there'll be a few bottles – will be uncorked, breathing. I need to get a move on... But Scotland's a small country and in a surprisingly short time I'm past Perth, over the bridge, through the capital and heading east along the coast.

The speed limit drops coming into the little town of Aberlady where Lord Elcho, The London Scottish Golf Club's founder, the commanding officer of the London Scottish Rifle Volunteers, is buried in the churchyard. Living in London I often golfed at The London Scottish. It has a military history and an unusual dress code: players wear a red shirt or pullover. The members being Anglo Scots, you might think the red was chosen to match the colour of their eyes. In fact, their conspicuous appearance is for the safety of the city's pedestrians who roam the bunkerless fairways. Those walkers and their dogs are all the hazards the course needs. It was laid out by Willie Dunn who was the US Open champion in 1894 when it was a matchplay competition. The following year, officially the first year of the event, he was runner-up when the format changed to strokeplay. So he's something of a forgotten Scottish golfing hero, but his work on Wimbledon Common ensures his good name lives on amongst the golfers of London postcode SW19.

Golf's been played at Wimbledon -- as it was at Black-heath in London – since the reign of James VI. Back then Wimbledon was an untamed wilderness full of highwaymen, prizefighters and even duellists. But by 1864 when the soldiers of the London Scottish Rifle Volunteers, who were posted nearby, informally established The London Scottish Golf Club, the common was becoming safer, more like the public park it is now. Soon golfers were competing in monthly medals and membership was opened to local residents. But tensions ran high between civilian and military fraternities in the club, not least because despite being outnumbered the club president would always be the regimental commanding officer with right of veto on all decisions.

After much argument and little settlement (specifically following a general meeting which - no surprise to present day golf club committee members - took three months to conclude) civilians and military went their separate ways, resulting in two clubs playing almost adjacent courses: the London Scottish Golf Club and The Royal Wimbledon Golf Club (which is actually the superior course, thanks to Harry Colt).

Tensions also ran high between walkers and golfers. Disputes between them led to regulations about how far off line a shot could deviate. A long draw, or worse a hook, could be illegal. Imagine the first tee nerves. A shank wouldn't just mean social shame. It might mean legal proceedings. Eventually these laws were replaced with the more straightforward, Tiger on day four, "red coat rule."

Today's clubhouse still suggests something of the club's military beginnings. The 19th century lockers are basically rifle cabinets and the bar still serves the regiment's dram of choice, Hodden Grey.

The club takes its history seriously. Club matches are played against the regimental golfing society and the pipes can be heard throughout the year, at the club supper, at Hogmanay and when the new captain drives himself in. They can be heard on Burns night too when the captain, no matter his nationality, wears the kilt.

In the tradition of the best Scottish courses it's windswept, natural and difficult. And it's a special treat, for the historically minded, revealing something of the early Scottish golfing missionaries to England. Wimbledon Common, even allowing for the excellent Royal Wimbledon Golf Club, is not strictly golfing country. But high above London, for some Scots, it's a little piece of home. The greens and tees are always in excellent condition, but the bits between are unremarkable because it's common land. It's up and down with few flat lies. It's also short, but not one for nervous golfers because trees line every hole and the walkers, who have right of way, can hinder play.

These days the London Scottish shares its course

with another club, The Wimbledon Common Golf Club. The Wimbledon Common Club plays out from the London Scottish's 10th hole, Caesar's Camp, while the London Scottish's first hole is the Common Club's 10th, a very long par-3 named after another military leader, their founder, Elcho. He golfed between the ages of 14 and 93 and died at 96.

Accelerating out of Aberlady, Lord Elcho's last resting place, and rounding the bay, heading into Gullane itself, the golf gets really good. It's a charming village which has given itself up to golf, more than anywhere else perhaps, including even Pinehurst and St Andrews. It's not just home to Gullane Golf Club's numbered and graded trinity: Course No.1 (1884), No.2 (1898) and No.3 (1910). It's also the home of mighty Muirfield, the prestigious and perfect Luffness New, Tom Doak's fabulous Renaissance Course and the two lovely tree-lined linksy layouts at Archerfield.

The Hawg's on Cuvee Training Camp. He's an excellent amateur sportsman, too old to sensibly carry on playing contact team sports, but still able to get his competitive fix from distance running and now golf. Most men, most animals, have an instinct to hunt and fight. Like all instincts it demands expression, but we can't have too much of it in civilised societies. So sport becomes a way to sublimate such inclinations. The Hawg once did this on the rugby pitch. But the years have forced him off the field and onto the fairways. His game's improving, but he's come to it a bit

late. He's not going to win many momentous tournaments, but like all involved, he's tilting at glory in
an annual buddy-trip which is more high-jinx than
high-quality golf, a much anticipated annual weekend with old friends from university. It's coming up at
the end of the month.

As hoped for, that night at dinner there's wine (much)
and steaks (sizeable, bloody). But at 8am next morning we're making our way down the opening hole of
Gullane No.3.

The courses here wend up, over and around Gullane
Hill. The turf is tight. The air is clear. The joy un-
bridled (as a golfing poet laureate once said). No.3 is
a fascinating course, a fun course, even a great one.
It asks interesting things of those who play here.
It doesn't ask for distance. Tom Doak believes the
greens on No.3 are the finest set of putting surfaces
he's ever seen. Many would agree. They're small, slick
and sloping, more than making up for the course's
modest length.

The 15th hole, 176 yards steeply downhill, is where
The Hawg's father, Bill, once successfully reached the
green with a single blow from his putter. Along with
his brothers, Douglas and Brian, they made a sometime ritual of this, putting from the tee.

I never met The Hawg's father. Apparently he was a
giant of a man, a colossus of rugby, so perhaps it was
easy for him, just a little flick. He ran the Scottish
Rugby Union through two Grand Slam winning cam-

paigns. I remember that a friend once borrowed his kilt. That friend was 6 foot 3 but the kilt still came halfway down his calves.

We take our mid-irons, both missing the green, and then, in memorium, we have a go with our putters, both falling short. It's a bit of a roller-coaster to get to the green. Some luck is required. Many, apparently, try this shot regularly. Putting from the tee, not a euphemism for anything else.

Back at the house there are voicemails to check, calls to return, emails to ignore. And then, after lunch, there's time for a snooze. Hey, we're 40 years old. The East Lothian sea breezes are enervating.

There's more golf in the afternoon and those sea breezes are suddenly strong winds and Course No.2 is a real challenge. Out at its furthest reaches the world is good. It's like a picture a child might draw: fairways streaming everywhere up and down hills; people golfing and walking; massive dunes; marshlands; the sea; a city and a castle framed by rocky hills; mighty mountains in the distance; a colossal suspension bridge far off; little towns and villages and roads; across the firth the Kingdom of Fife; in the sky fast moving clouds and aircraft coming into land at Edinburgh airport.

Despite these great distractions we play to our handicaps. It's only average scoring, our own average scoring, but in the windy conditions it feels like a cause for celebration.

Every golfer knows that, whatever they've scored, it might have been better but could have been worse. Most golfers, unless they're on a serious upwards trajectory, are happy to play to their handicap. This is instructive. Progress isn't everything. It might be a worldwide obsession, the raison d'etre of modern times. But sometimes there's much to be said for stability, for the status quo. We want to hit the ball further. We want to eliminate the spin which has an adverse effect on our shots. We want to score low and make more money and look younger. But where will it all end? At some stage, for a while at least, we may need to accept things as they are. Perhaps we'll even be forced to turn back the clock. Nobody wants to see Gullane's shorter courses, No.2 and No.3, become meaningless.

This is probably about more than just golf distance technology. The 21st century seems to involve increasingly extreme weather conditions. Ice storms in Augusta killed off Ike's tree (the loblolly pine Eisenhower wanted removed in 1956 before the committee overruled him). In California the cypresses which narrow the landing area on the 18th at Pebble have bent and broken in freak storms. Much of the 17th fairway at Rosses Point in Ireland, beloved of Loyal and Pat, is gone for good, returned to whence it came. In England those tees at Royal West Norfolk which overlook The Wash cling on by a thread. It may be nothing to do with manmade climate change. But sometimes progress isn't all it's cracked up to be.

Sometimes going forwards is to go backwards.

Rock armour and gabions hold dune systems in place. But man cannot forever tether time and tide. The golf industry is busy developing golf balls that will travel 300 yards off the face of a half-hit 9-iron. Where do these guys get off? Soon we'll all be putting from the tee.

In all walks of life we hear that progress is unassailable. We just sit back and wait for The Singularity. The future is a nightmare of human suffering, robot rule and man's eventual extinction... And worse still our golf courses are becoming dated.

Gullane's been good and bad to me. I first came here more than 20 years ago and met a bookish brunette with a stylish haircut. That was good. The following day I played Course No.1 for the first time and shot a shocking, but memorable, 100. That was bad. No doubt my mind was on higher things. I was slicing, shanking, swooning probably.

After that I spent a lot of time here. I'd often come down from Aberdeen and stay with my new girlfriend at her flat in Marchmont, Edinburgh. In the evenings I'd walk her across Bruntsfield Links to her job as an usher at The King's Theatre. (Bruntsfield Links: one of the earliest known golfing sites – perhaps the first known inland golf site - where still, in the summer, right in the middle of the city, at no cost, golfers can play on truly ancient ground, modestly maintained, though now no more than a pitch and putt.) And we'd often take the bus to Gullane to visit her mum and walk on the beach and go for dinner in The Old Clubhouse. It really was the old clubhouse, built in the 19th century but put to other uses since the 1920s when the golfers outgrew it. The Hawg's grandfather owned this place for a while in the 60s, running it in one of its earlier incarnations as a restaurant.

Inevitably The Hawg and I manage a few drinks there, a few drinks elsewhere too, so that next morning, in high winds and biting rain, we choose not to play No.1 but instead to avail ourselves of some golf history, courtesy of Archie Baird who runs his brilliant little museum from a room adjacent to the club professional's shop.

It's pleasant to think that an ingenious St Andrean shepherd once inverted his crook and took a swipe at a pebble and, lo and behold, the game of golf was born, just as growing up in Greenock I believed the town's most famous son, James Watt, once looked at a boiling kettle and the extinction event known as the industrial revolution began. But things are never so simple. And it seems the Scots merely perfected golf and steam engines, rather than invented them outright.

That's what we learn from Archie's whirlwind history of the game which he delivers with aplomb and, crucially, with props.

We begin in Holland, almost 500 years ago. Archie says the Dutch didn't exactly develop the game, nor did they keep it going. But they played something akin to golf and they played it on ice. They played towards a target, a stake in the ice, not a hole: it wasn't fishing. It was 'koff.'

It was Scottish wool merchants who brought the game to the British Isles. They had a lucrative market in Holland, a country which was too flat and wet for raising sheep. With an unfavourable wind they were sometimes forced to stay in Holland for days or weeks, entertaining themselves, often with 'koff.'

We look at a painting which Archie describes as the iconic connection between this early Dutch game and Scottish golf. It's by Adriaen Van de Velde and was painted in 1668. It shows Haarlem Cathedral and a windmill which still stands today and there, in the foreground, addressing the ball, is a guy wearing a kilt. The Dutch didn't wear kilts and this man is either a Scottish wool trader or a mercenary soldier (a lot of Scots made for foreign ports and fought for whoever would pay them). Archie says that the clubs in the painting were probably Scottish. In Scotland there was beech wood for heads and ash for shafts, plenty of each.

Around this time Scottish bow makers were at something of a loose end because firearms had recently been invented. Some turned their attention to producing golf clubs, lighter and lovelier things than some of the basic contraptions which were first used. It was a skilful operation and the long nosed clubs they created are beautiful, delicate but strong, with their sheepskin grips, ash shafts, beech heads and protective leading edge and sole plate made from sheep's horn. I long to swing one. But I'm lucky enough to hold one, gripping and regripping and taking half a stance in the manner of a bloke in suit and tie sizing up golf clubs in a department store. Hawg says it's like giving a chimpanzee a Samurai sword.

The head was connected to the shaft by intricately splicing the wood, then gluing, finally tying with fishing line. To get the swing weight right – the heft, they called it - they scooped out some wood and added lead. There was no custom fitting. It's just a craftsman's sense of optimum balance, a carefully calibrated fragment of poetry.

Archie, it turns out, is a little bit of living history himself. Well, his wife is. Her Great Grandfather is Willie Park Sr., a four times Open Champion, and her great uncle is Willie Park Jr, designer of Gullane No.2 and No.3.

Archie basically married into golfing aristocracy. This was before he knew much about golf, let alone golf memorabilia. This wasn't a Hollywood actor marrying the daughter of a pop icon he modelled himself on! Sheila wasn't the crowning item in his golf collection. But she was the start of his interest in the game. Everything, he says, just fell into place.

"We were newly married and I'd inherited a basement flat in the middle of Edinburgh, on York Place. It had been used as an air raid shelter in the war. My mother lived in style upstairs but my wife and I got the basement, a great big basement. It needed furniture so we scoured the lane sales all over the city and the junk shops too."

One day at a lane sale, all furniture and bric-a-brac arranged on the street, he saw a couple of old golf bags with some long-nosed clubs in them. He rubbed the dust off them and saw the legend, W Park. He said to Sheila, "these clubs are made by your grandfather and nobody wants them!" He bought a whole bag for 10 shillings. Realising the skill that had gone into them he wanted more. Every junk shop in Edinburgh had lots of them. "But soon they realised I was buying them and the bastards raised their prices to a pound!"

Golf, he explains, began to grow popular in Scotland. "It was a game played by posh people while the caddies carried clubs. But the beautiful thing was they played alternate shots, foursomes. Nobody marked a card. It was a convivial affair, mostly for the well-to-do, and there was the serious business of some heavy betting on the side.

"In this way the game was kept going – always the foursomes format - mostly played just on a small number of courses up and down the east coast as well as on a smaller number of inland spots. Then in 1850 the revolution happened: the gutta percha ball, gutta being a tropical gum like rubber, except it could be moulded. It changed golf forever, allowing it to go worldwide. At Gullane it allowed them to take the game up onto the hill. With the feathery they simply played seven holes laid out on the flat. The new ball meant height and distance were more possible and courses became more audacious."

Then in 1860 The Open Championship began and at the same time another revolution: strokeplay golf.

"By 1900 there were 2,300 courses worldwide. Ten years later there were 4,000 courses, really because of the change of ball, something which was finally affordable and durable."

Archie reckons a feathery ball, a pristine one, will sell for roughly £5,000. The ones he has on display are perhaps less valuable, well-worn, handled by all who visit his museum. The earliest gutta-percha balls are here too, probably made in nearby Musselburgh. The early smooth ones didn't fly well, but as they developed nicks and grazes they took to the air. Soon patterns were being hand hammered onto them, squares and circles, adopted or abandoned according to their success. The gutta ball was eventually replaced too, wiped out by American rubber core balls at the start of the 20th Century, specifically the Haskell ball, stuffed full of hundreds of feet of elastic.

We're talked and walked through a complete timeline of golf clubs as well, wooden ones for featheries, new iron ones for rubber balls with strange markings on the face, modest lines at first, then various adventurous ones, including a crazy standout with vertical grooves, not good for slicers and hookers...

Soon they were getting heavier with thick brass plates on the bottom. Progress isn't always linear. These clubs are far less wieldy than the beautiful work of the bowmakers.

But there's an explanation. Builders would cross the links to get sand from the beach and their heavy carts left scars on the fairways. So the industrial sole plate was needed to play from this rough road, hence the brassie. What about if the ball's in a deep wheel rut? There were no local rules for this but there was a rut iron, impossibly small. Only God could hit it...

A golfer would need amazing skills to achieve any success with some of the tiny and eccentric club-faces on display. The waterfall iron, with its flowing grooves, looks impossible to hit. And a giant sand iron, like a dinner plate, seems only a little less use-less, unless perhaps you were frying eggs. (It wasn't until Gene Sarazen that we had what anyone might recognise as a modern sand iron.)

The variety, seemingly, is endless. People began to carry more and more clubs. There were no limits on numbers. So, bags were soon used. Caddies only had two hands after all. (And they often went barefoot.) We look at an early stand bag from about 1890. It's kind of incredible and it's still working.

It's the American inventions though which seem most to usher in the modern age. Hickory shafts and

Persimmon heads begin to look more like the clubs we all now know and use. Persimmon wood meant there was no need for splicing. This fruit wood is very hard so you can bore a hole into it. These socket headed clubs, not spliced, meant a more elegant finish, something which could be more readily mass-produced.

But hickory - mostly from the Carolinas - is of limited supply and so people turned to various metals for their shafts. There was a certain shame attached to this, a little like the feelings one might have when pulling out a giant driver in front of a golfer who remembers well teeing off with a clubhead just bigger than the ball. There was a solution though to this unwelcome modernity. Steel shafts were painted to look like wood.

We look at some golf clubs from Ben Sayers, amongst them the first designs to be patented, now standard practise for all manufacturers. Sayers was an acrobat turned professional golfer who'd celebrate a great shot with an airborne somersault. Sayers' caddy, Archie tells us gleefully, was Big Crawford, a man who would stand no nonsense. "That's the rule and there's the referee" he'd tell dissenters, showing them his Big Bertha sized-fist.

Finally, Archie shows us an aluminium headed driver. They didn't really take off till the 1980s but this one dates from 1930. "When the metal clubs came in I began to lose interest," Archie says.

It's the most amazing collection. And, shared with us by its expert curator, it's an unforgettable experience.

Ben Crenshaw officially opened this little museum – The Heritage of Golf - in 1980. He's a serious golf collector himself, books mostly, a great golfer who's probably more in love with the game as a whole than that narrow part of it which is professional tour golf. Archie tells us he sent Ben a stiff letter after his team's ill-mannered and early celebrations at Brookline following a remarkable final day comeback in the 1990 Ryder Cup. Archie's interest – like Ben's – is the whole game. Anyway, they're all friends again now.

The tour over, we head for the clubhouse. The Hawg and I are on coffees and I'd put money on Archie ordering a Kummel, the totemic drink of golfers at traditional clubs (Prestwick and Royal County Down being the institutions which take it most seriously). But Archie orders a John Panton, named after a Scottish golfer who had a long and significant career, playing well into old age. He had a couple of close-runs in The Open Championship and played in three Ryder Cups. He was also honorary professional to The R&A. 'Gentleman' John Panton had been a great golfer but, as the prefix suggests, his manners were the thing. Archie again uses the word 'convivial' when we talk about him. The drink named after him is made by pouring angostura bitters round the glass then filling with ginger beer and a dash of lime cordial.

To have a drink named after you is no small compliment. That it's non-alcoholic – but with a tasty kick – adds some charm. The Hawg says it's a favourite of a great mutual friend, a man on the wagon for a few years now and a member at nearby Luffness New. Archie tells us it's a popular drink at golf clubs across Scotland, a marker of a gentleman's credentials if he knows the drink, a guide to a barman's knowledge if he makes it without further guidance.

Arnold Palmer is venerated in similar style. An Arnold Palmer is the old Southern half and half, iced tea and lemonade. John Daly enjoys the same adulation, with vodka added. He didn't get the joke at first. It was a trademark infringement, he said. But now he's got the official version to market he probably sees some fun in it.

Tony Jacklin apparently often orders The Tony Jacklin at his club in Florida. He'll live forever as a US and British Open winner, a great Ryder Cup captain and a true gentleman. But I'm sure he's almost equally tickled that a club sandwich bears his name.

Some golfers, yet to be so honoured, have taken matters into their own hands. Nicklaus, Player, Norman, Els and Faldo are amongst a number who have bought up vineyards or at least signed-off on licensing arrangements to see their names appear on wine labels. No doubt it makes for great business. But the ambition must always be to achieve such fame spontaneously.

This is what we should all aim for. The Hawg and I will never be remembered as guys who shot consecutive 65s in Open qualifying. And nobody sensible really wants to be remembered for drinking first-growth Clarets on school nights. But anyone would like to live on as a refreshment, or failing that as something to eat, a snack or a light lunch, say.

Archie was a pilot during the war. His training finished after the battle of Arnhen in 1944 where all the glider pilots had been shot down. So Archie found himself volunteering to take their place, to fly massive gliders carrying troops deep into Europe beyond The Rhine as The Allies made their final push across the continent.

After the war, with a friend, an art student turned air-gunner who had beaten the odds and survived three tours of combat, they took off to Paris on a motorbike. They sold tea and coffee they'd taken with them and managed to stay for a month. Visiting the great galleries in Paris was the beginning of a lifelong interest in art, specifically painting.

"Paintings can charm you. I've loved collecting clubs. And I've enjoyed collecting books, first the books which helped me identify the clubs, then more general golf titles. But you get fed up with them. My wife bought me my first golf painting and it turned my head. It took me back to Paris."

We talk about Henry Raeburn, a great Scottish artist,

a golfer too, and occasionally a golf artist. We talk about Rembrandt's sketch of a golfer. It shows a man with a colossal snow shovel of a golf club. It predates the Van De Velde which shows the Scotsman golfing on the Dutch ice with the lovely long-nosed clubs.

The Golfers by Charles Lees is explained to us, perhaps the most important of all early golf paintings. Archie owns a head and shoulders in oil, one of the studies Lees did for the painting. It's of William Mephibosheth Goddard, a member of The Honourable Company. Archie checked the middle name with his minister. Mephibosheth was a lame boy who had claim to David's throne. Archie reckons this gentleman golfing superstar had some congenital disorder or maybe a club foot, but it didn't stop him winning the silver medal five times, once with the lowest ever score at Musselburgh.

Archie is in possession of a number of serious golf artworks. One sketch, which he bought for £250, had been loaned out to an international touring exhibition and was insured for £40,000. But it's the John Smart works which he loves most. Smart was a Scottish landscape painter, probably best known for his 20 watercolours, 'The Golfing Greens of Scotland', painted in the 1880s and 90s, delicate yet often dramatic. Collectively they are beseeching.

Archie actually owns a number of the originals, including - following a high-value swap - Smart's watercolour of Gullane. Engravings of all 20 are in the clubhouse there: Musselburgh, St Andrews, Carnoustie, Troon, Bruntsfield, Prestwick, Stirling, North Berwick, Montrose, Gullane, Luffness, Dunbar, Leven, Perth, Machrihanish, Lanark, Aberdeen, Elie, Glasgow and Leith.

Many of us feel that golf has meaning. It perhaps doesn't have a meaning, singular. But that litany of courses - some of them no more, some of them still at the forefront of modern golf - is enough to convince me that the game has substance.

Archie furnishes us with a final quote:

"A tolerable day, a tolerable green, a tolerable opponent supply, or ought to supply, all that any reasonably constituted human being should require in the way of entertainment. With a fine sea view and a clear course in front of him, the golfer may be excused if he regards golf, even though it be indifferent golf, as the true and adequate end of man's existence."

This is from the very collectible Badminton Edition of Golf, put together by Arthur Balfour in 1890. First edition, ex-libris Archie Baird, I'm guessing.

We are sent on our way, Archie insisting we make one final climb up the hill to take a look down the 7th fairway of Gullane Number 1 and over to Muirfield in the east. The view is gobsmacking and that drive down the 7th is tantalising. I'm no John Daly or Samuel Messieux (he once hit a feathery ball 361 yards) but stood there on the tee – without my clubs admittedly - I'm sure I could make the green...

Anyway, it's all over. The 400-yard downhill drive will have to wait. Hawg's got a full exercise programme and I have a long trip home, 500 miles south. It's been great though, illuminating and inspiring. There've been no actual signs or visions. We don't deserve such enlightenment. But we'll remember the golf on Gullane Hill and our time with Archie Baird.

15 OLD FRIENDS, 3910

Humans have roamed the earth in small groups since earliest times, following migrating animals and seeking better things, finer weather, improved conditions. We gathered and we hunted (or vice versa). But in more recent times we've settled down because we've harnessed nature, at least learned to grow crops and domesticate and farm animals. Deep inside though, on some level, most of us still yearn for older ways, the open road. It's part of our make-up, that in small groups we should move on and move up. One day this buried instinct will materialise again and we will perhaps rise out of our atmosphere and beyond the solar system in search of new worlds. Small exploratory ships will lead the way, small groups of space explorers going boldly, maybe each carrying a bag of weapons, light-sabres which paint a perfect parabola, swung in the face of an alien enemy. Until that time though, we simply make do. We must fulfil our deepest desires and express our individual bravery with a somewhat muted version of hunting in the Milky Way and further. I'm thinking, inevitably, of the 'buddy trip.'

To the English speakers of the British Isles a 'buddy trip' sounds like a shallow rite of passage. We don't really do 'buddies.' They're for Americans. Consequently, we don't have a generic name for these all-important annual jaunts. If they're formal they might be a 'society.' The informal ones must live without a collective noun, but most of them do have some sort of sobriquet. I've got friends who live and die by their yearly get-together, a Ryder-Cup format affair played between those who reside in the east of the country and those in the west. They call it 'The Stryder Cup.' For my part, I'm involved with a competition we imagine to be eternal, more glorious than The Amateur Championship or The Open. For reasons best known to its founders it's 'The Cuvée Classic.' It goes with a swing, many swings, in fact.

Al, Bob, Cameron, Christian, Craig, Mark, Neil, Nick, Richie, Roger, Steve, Tom, Tony and occasional others, get together each year at a time and a place agreed by email consensus but organised by the previous year's champion. There's no small glory in winning, but there is a price to pay: arranging things for the following year. This involves fixing dates, which means hundreds of emails and a complicated spreadsheet necessitated by individuals' domestic arrangements and commitments which only increase as we get older. Every effort is made to exclude no-one who wishes to attend: 'leave no man,' they say. It also involves the tricky business of finding the ideal location, placating the Anglo-Scots one year, the Scottish citizenry the next. Even more than this, the winner will typically spend much of their victorious year photographing the Cuvée Classic cocktail shaker in various locations, held aloft beside the Taj Mahal or The Eifel Tower or propped up on a random bar somewhere in Glasgow. It's no small task. I know that when he wins The Hawg books extravagant holidays to far-flung places, just him, his long-suffering girlfriend and the trophy. Then photos are carefully shared across whatever social media stream is current. Many man hours are lost to Whatscrap or Faceboast. Massive email streams eat into our working days and as the event comes closer the large number of out-of-office auto-responses we see on Fridays tell me that people are hitting the course.

And we're not alone. Across Britain, and indeed the world, groups of golfers are similarly silly, or committed, as we like to think of it. The UK's GDP probably suffers because of this. Potential medical breakthroughs are being undermined.

Despite the heavy price the winner pays in administrative efforts, which include having the trophy engraved, victory is always sweet. It's quite a thing to take home that cheap cocktail shaker of no particular beauty or intricate craftsmanship, but carved with the names of past champions, from Steve Philip, the inaugural winner, to others who have prevailed, be it Steve's brother, Cameron, or multiple winners, Al Hogg, Christian Bruce or Tom Jeffery (whose name once appears on the prize as Tom Jaffarey, a testicular joke made when he failed to have the trophy inscribed and so the next year's holder did it for him). The quality of the engravings is, like the golf, mixed. Various ironmongers and cobblers have done dreadful work down the years.

In this time of anxiety, global stress and political change – none of which is ever discussed 'on Cuvée' - the buddy trip is a tonic, a time to play some golf and relax with friends who – probably – we've not seen for a year. It gives us perspective, frames the year, allows us – a little – to see ourselves as others see us. If one old friend has put on some weight and aged noticeably, chances are we have too.

In this better modern world where men are as involved domestically as women are, it's also a rare chance to go off with the guys and do, for one whole weekend, what our fathers might have done every Saturday: relax and unwind.

And because these people are friends, real friends forged in the fire of hard-fought-for time away from home, it's always easy and relaxed when we get together.

Cuvée begins on a Friday, a light lunch, some drinks and golf. We have our first tee photos taken, stood in line, each with a random club pulled from our bags so that looking back we might think Roger actually was taking to the first tee of Royal Aberdeen with a wedge or Richie with a putter or Neil with an umbrella (and, in fact, it might have been better if they had). I look at these photo from down the years and I see a phalanx of bankers and accountants and gardeners and publicists (amazing how it works out for some and not others) and none of us is getting any younger.

First tee nerves are not a thing. Perhaps they are in grander groups, more formal competitions. But they're yet to be recognised at Cuvée, not least because Friday counts for nothing. It's a mere warm-up. I want to question this, especially because my Friday record is superb. But I know that the meaningless Friday is now a tradition. It can't be changed. I also know, with a heavy heart, that my Friday record is only so good precisely because it counts for nothing. It's a record which does me no favours, partly because handicaps can be adjusted for competition day according to Friday performances.

The Friday evening will be dinner, drinking and even dancing, though less drinking than there used to be when we'd be heading into nightclubs at 2am, more dining than there once was when we were younger and slimmer, and almost no dancing nowadays either. Actually, in recent times – in our 40s – there has been a return to varying degrees of svelteness. Mortality encroaches and long-distance running is not uncommon in this demographic, healthy-eating too. I've seen green teas ordered as bedtime approaches. Some even renounce alcohol entirely, having had more than their fair share in previous years. We used to be a drinking society with a golfing problem, but things change. We're older and ostensibly wiser. Reckless abandon is mostly in the past. The only drug which makes much sense is the green opium.

Golf is the thing now, becoming more and more popular amongst us. It used to be, really, that I was the only one who truly loved the game. For others, well, they played golf only because they were Scottish and they put themselves through this weekend for the wild fun of it. Golf was probably insufficiently masculine for a few of these guys when they were younger, or at least they had other sports to focus on. Too old for rugby now, a few of these Scots are finally fulfilling their genetic destinies, joining the golf clubs of East Lothian, drinking John Pantons. A bit like folk music and country music, it gets most of us in the end.

The reverse is also true though, with some golfing less and less as real life intrudes. That's kind of the case for me. It's also true of Steve and Cameron, St Andrews brothers and regular Cuvée champions in its early days, now no longer fulfilling their geographic destiny and getting worse as the years go on!

On the Saturday morning I am in a hotel room dreaming. I am dreaming of golf. The man in the bed next to me is dreaming of golf. We must wake. We must wash. The Cuvée is to be decided today. We must eat breakfast and recover. We each must phone home and tell our children that their daddy is alive.

The first tee is no place for a hangover, but there's always a hangover or six or seven. That opening shot, on competition day, with an audience, might be testing unless we remember to forget the audience and trust ourselves. You can't be scared or intimidated amongst friends (or else you can be). But ignore the paranoia and be secure and confident because it's only fun. Typically, there are a few reasonable shots and a few rotten ones. But soon the games are on the course and, in threes or fours we are side by side, walking in the same direction.

There are various forms of social solidarity: paying income tax; doing charitable work; helping out at the kids' school; being understanding with neighbours who think the parking spaces on the road outside their home belong to them (ok, not that one). They're all important and I'm varyingly committed to them all. But there's one I'm wholly committed to: annual golf tours with friends.

This is the story we tell each other, that there is a thing we do and we call it golf and it means something and we do it together each year when we travel to a different location and decide our champion and celebrate him for the rest of the year, letting him sign off his emails as 'champ' and addressing the others as 'chumps' and 'losers' and so in this way we are a group, a society. It makes me happy. It makes us all happy.

But golf's meaning is not in the happiness it provides. Golf's meaning is more likely to be found in the substance it gives us, the way it shapes our lives. I read somewhere that having kids doesn't necessarily make us happy, but it does give us meaning, which is all we really need. Suicide is not readily committed by those who are unhappy. It's those who feel their lives lack meaning who are most likely to cut them unnaturally short.

Our get-together gives us some meaning, not in any imperative way, but it's a consolation nonetheless. Golf gives us meaning. It needn't be golf, but it works for me. I sometimes clean my clubs and polish my shoes (ok, it's rare that I do either of those things, but I could and many do.) However, I do keep course guides, read golf books, write golf books. I consume (and instantly forget) swing tips. I practise my swing, clubless, in front of mirrors and windows. I fill idle moments with thoughts of sweet shots. I imagine how, in future, I might become better or play such and such a course. And here, it's the reason for meeting friends. Honestly, I could fail to phone a single friend for years. As a grown up I don't bother with chit chat so much. But I will, still, sometimes, make an arrangement. And golf is always a good arrangement, a thing to pursue.

Golf can be highly social. For all the faux moments of transcendence I imagine on my own on a hill in Perthshire or beside The Wash in Norfolk, golf with new friends is fun (everyone's a friend once you've golfed with them) and golf with old friends is best of all.

But the relaxation can't last forever on Cuvée Saturday. The hangovers wear off, but we're intoxicated, in high spirits. And some holes in, we are getting a sense of who's playing well, who's looking like a winner. Someone calls over from an adjoining hole: "The Bruce has had five straight pars, a birdie and one bogey." A dagger in my heart.

Playing alone it's all too easy. Without an audience, with nothing on the line, your finer sporting qualities step forward. With your friends, with something at stake, a less talented golfer is suddenly playing on your behalf. Which one is real? Are you real, when you're alone? Or are you really only the person others see through the prism of competition?

I notice myself swinging a little short, a little slow, then a little fast. Mostly though I settle into the game and forget about the glories on offer. My swing lengthens and improves. Instead of duffing the ball around, I begin to produce reasonable shots.

Control is everything. I'm always telling my American friends about gun control, my catholic friends about birth control and my golfing friends about self-control. The golfer must control the ball, but first the golfer must control himself. This self-control requires self-knowledge. You are solely responsible for the shots you hit and sometimes that's hard to take. Know your limitations, what you are able to do, what you might be able to do, sometimes... With practise, one can expand those limitations.

To become a passable golfer one should have some confidence, but have no self-regard because that must surely be punctured sooner rather than later with a mishit, as happens to me on the 12th, a double bogey and no points.

"Brucie's had another birdie," we hear. I get a feeling this won't be my year.

Once I was victorious in the Cuvée, with 36 points at The Belfry. (That stuffy, suburban place between midlands motorways really fired me up, bringing back the great golfing moments of so many VHS tapes, Seve and Olly and Sandy and Woosie.) 36 points doesn't seem like much of a score, but I played well. And, of course, in the UK, handicaps are not about your average round but about your potential, so 36 points, sometimes less, is often enough for a Cuvée triumph.

A few moments still stick in the mind from that weekend. On 10 – the famous short par-4 over water where Seve unbelievably hit the green and where, as with the sub-four-minute-mile, everyone soon started to do the same thing – I stuck a three-wood straight over the pin. Exhilarated by history, it must have been the biggest three-wood I've ever hit. Then on 11 I hit a meaty drive. Roger, who by his own ad-mission knows little about golf, looked at me when I reached the ball. "Is that your second to there?" he asked. I was so pleased: he might as well have been David Leadbetter complimenting my swing. When you hit a great shot you imagine it will stay with you, a shot to call on, readily repeatable, for the rest of the round, for many rounds perhaps, for the rest of your life. But a few holes later I was playing poorly, thinking ahead to what might be, dreaming impossible dreams, and it's a drive on 17 which I best remember, a drive so bad it could have cost me the Cuvée, no less... Somehow I got a passable shot away on the last, and a good second up to the green too, not exactly the Christy O'Connor 2-iron I had in my mind, yet good enough to lift the cocktail shaker. But that penultimate drive – I knew it then – was nasty. Good luck getting that one out of your head, I'd thought, in a cruel self-harming, self-fulfillingly prophetic sort of a way. Sure enough, ever since, my driving's been off. I've never been long. I don't and can't hit it hard. But I was straight, a little draw. I was never crooked. But the bigger the club and the longer the shaft and the older I've got the worse it's become. And I put it down to that moment at The Belfry. The horror of self-reflection: it was cowardliness, I now realise, the fear of winning a little thing amongst friends, that brought about a long-term reversal of fortune in my driving. And biblically it was pride – the tee shot on the 10th and Roger's accidental compliment on the 11th – that came before the fall.

(It was Roger I once golfed with at that most prestigious of Spanish clubs, Valderamma, on the Marbella estate. We were guests because I was writing a travel feature or two for Scottish newspapers and we were on best behaviour, except that on the pristine practise ground, under the watchful eye of the club's director of golf, our host, Roger tried, with explosive effect, to take the top one off a pyramid of balls with his 7-iron. It was a joke, a good joke in retrospect. It reflects well on him and badly on me because I'd told him not to change his shoes in the car-park. He didn't like this pettiness and it was payback!)

But all that was years ago. This time round my driving's quite straight but we keep hearing about Brucie's exploits up ahead. And then suddenly Hogg's in the mix too. "He's going along really nicely," is the call.

The guys I'm playing with think I may yet have enough points to win the thing. They've fallen away, but there's some small pleasure in having someone in your own group win and I feel their support. In some ways this makes it harder. They're watching me, I think. Golf, like writing, is ok when it's strangers watching, strangers reading the words. But I'm more inclined to choke when it's friends. I can't write if I think about friends and family reading the output.

Anyway, I keep getting the drives away and the irons on or nearly on. At the 16th, tired of waiting while Bruce and Hogg mess around ahead, we take our chances and play. They're out of range. It's not a dangerous situation. But a really good ball might make it over the saddle and trundle down the fairway into their vicinity. I hit a really good ball. Tom does too. When we get to our shots we find they have been decorated in black pen. 'I am a twat,' they read.

Amongst friends this sort of stuff can be hilarious, less so in the re-telling perhaps. Certainly, it was enough to ensure much laughter for the final holes, none of which I could par, suffering from my own sniggers whenever I addressed the ball. You had to be there. It's the joy of the golf trip, only understandable in the moment amongst friends.

In the clubhouse Cameron's laptop is produced. There's some tension in the air as he inputs the scores and Stableford points are tallied while he sips a beer. I always worry he might spill his drink, drown his computer and we'll never know the winner and decades of our statistics might be lost. But he's got a steady hand and, as a management consultant, he probably backs up. Down the years his showmanship has increased and his reverse order read-out is worth the price of entry.

The first name called receives a large wooden spoon. It's meant to be kept in his golf bag for the rest of the year, shaming him whenever he plays. In fact, it's no hardship for Tony who has become its owner. He almost never plays these days, having fallen far, in golfing-terms, from the useful mid-teens handicapper I used to golf with at Aberdeen more than 20 years before, The Cuvée Classic being a get-together for old friends from that town's university. How can it be, I wonder, that he could be 80 or less over the ancient Kings Links or at Hazlehead or sometimes down the coast at Stonehaven? But golf's not like riding a bike. It's more involved, not that he's worried.

My name's read out all too soon, with two names still to come. I managed 36 points, my winning tally from years before. Were the game ahead to win by a point or two I'd blame their graffiti. In fact, Hogg managed 44 and Bruce 45. Record-breaking scores, unheard of in this group, smashing their handicaps.

There's always a long journey back to the hotel, some sort of traffic issue or wrong turning which allows us to feel inexplicably tired and to sceptically question the wisdom of the big night ahead. At some stage in the future we'll fail to muster in the bar: we'll be old men going to sleep. But that time has not yet come. Hogg, a veteran of countless rugby tours, has the kitty bag ready. "20s in please gentleman." That will be the refrain throughout the night.

Within a short time we will achieve the ideal of social intoxication. We will be blissfully content. Luckily this won't last long and we will push on into pointless and painful drunkenness. We are all winners.

The guys I know who play something similar, the east vs west Stryder Cup, say the actual weekend is not the only purpose of the thing. "The purpose is to simply get through it alive, maybe with some fun along the way depending on how ugly and intense the mood gets late at night," Tom tells me. "The joy it brings for the rest of the year, poring over the statistics and the pictures on the website, is almost as important as the 48-hours real-time in which it all takes place. The sustained bonds are fundamental."

Nick, the other Stryder Cup veteran I know, reckons, likewise, that the purpose is to make memories (or at least vague memories brought to life in photographs) which can be shared down the years. "It's about living through these annually occurring and undeniably special days and nights and perhaps, as the years go on, to be amongst the last men standing, looking back fondly on it all. The common sense of continuity means a lot."

Why do we bother golfing? It takes up much time. It costs so much money. We could be doing something better. I'm not sure that on my death bed I'll necessarily wish I'd played more golf. But, in the final analysis, when the paranoia and pain that follows these boozy weekends is gone, I almost always wish I could play more golf with friends.

Golf reveals truths in our friends. Some look good but when the scores are tallied it appears they have flattered to deceive. Others look less than useful but on the final count we learn they have been efficient and effective. We learn about ourselves too. In golfing with friends we go some way towards seeing ourselves as others see us. Golf itself probably isn't so revealing. But what you can bring to it and what others bring to it is.

We can all be clever on Twitter and beautiful on Instagram: online nobody knows if we're naked, many days removed from our last shave and shower. But on the golf course all is revealed. There's an honesty in open competition amongst comrades, revelling in our strengths and weaknesses together.

16 FLOW, 3450

On the course, at our best, we are inside ourselves, our very best selves. Things, within the limitations of our abilities and know-how, go smoothly and we play almost as well as we can. For some this lasts just a couple of shots, a hole or a run of holes. Sometimes the spell – because that's what it is, a kind of magic – lasts for half the round, an outward or inward half. It's why we often collect our thoughts on the 10th tee and give ourselves a stern talking to, knowing that a new nine is a chance to begin again, to work some sorcery, to find our inner calm. For the best players, as we know, this alchemy can last for a full round, even for a 72-hole tournament, though such things are rare. Typically, a top-flight golfer will have to endure at least one tournament round where they fall a little from grace, finding themselves back on earth scraping a couple of birdies and fighting for pars to hold their lead.

Most golfers never get close to such glories. But many

of us are familiar with the feeling where we are woken from the reverie, typically towards the end of a game as we realise we're looking at a score of some significance. That's often the thing that shatters the dream. It's why so many professionals refuse to look at scoreboards and, instead, play it one shot at a time, never looking up or out.

Why can't we stay in that place, maintaining that internal happiness and concentration, enjoying a purity of purpose? It's because of hopes and ambitions, reality dawning. We get distracted by details and desire.

Golf, I've noticed, almost more than any other game, gives us what we put into it. Without fail, every golfer I've met who is any good has played a lot, really put in the hours, worked with others too, taken lessons from experts. (And they have big hands. So many of the good golfers have such big hands!)

But not all golfers who put in the hours and attain excellence can attain tour status. A fair few regular golfers wield their sticks seemingly as well as some guys on tour but, when it comes down to it, they can't shoot really low, can't keep it together for long enough to make a living from the game. On the range, working quietly, you might mistake them for world beaters. Yet something is missing from their skill set. Maybe it's the short game, probably the putting. But often it's the ability to silence the world and zone in. And that's where the world's best spend a lot of their time: 'in the zone'.

All golfers have visited that place but few can find their way back to it on demand. It is an unmapped region of the brain. Of course, you don't have to be a golfer to have been there. In fact, playing golf is one of the trickier ways to experience it. After all, it's not easy to be in that state of flow when you're walking between shots, thinking about yardage, remembering wonky swing tips, foolishly considering what might go wrong, staring too long at the trees down the left, feeling anxious about the guys watching from the clubhouse terrace. It's easier to feel that quiet, joyful concentration when working alone without pressure. No doubt great writers find themselves there when they switch off their internet connection and stop counting the words. Artists will be in that space when they're silently, carefully at work with canvas and ink and the hours slip by. It might be experienced gardening, I suppose, or cleaning up. No doubt, however and whenever we experience it, the result is a beneficial break from the everyday. But for it to make a real difference, for it to confer advantage on someone, it must be experienced when performing a task which is best done naturally and creatively, a task where critical input is a distraction during it even if it is useful before and after it. That's certainly the case with golf and some other sports too.

But it's golf where getting into the moment seems toughest, probably because so little of the game is action and so much of it is walking and thinking (or talking and drinking). Other sports allow you to get into the zone because there's not so much time available for contemplation. In a game of association football or soccer the moments can fly by for the players as a team works together, automagically, doing their best without worrying about technique (unless they're in an England shirt in which case a collective panic ensues and basic skills are lost as a fear of failure takes hold). In tennis, sure, the player must serve to get the ball in play, but in any given rally the players will then let their talent and training take over. Snooker, a little like golf, is a game where technique is key and a stationary object must be made to move. But the small size of the table (compared to a golf course) allows the player to more readily find a rhythm and fall into time with it.

The great golfer will overcome all unsettling and nerve-wrangling difficulties and arrive in that delightfully tranquil domain of the mind. And all's well there, at least while the putts drop and the drives soar. Then though, a little rain falls on their parade - a small but costly misadventure in a bunker, a bad break, a gust of wind, a noise from the crowd - and they are unceremoniously returned to earth, where, as PG Wodehouse might have it, shots are lost because of 'the uproar of butterflies in adjoining meadows'. If flow is to be maintained such small aberrations must be ignored or overcome.

Some golf coaches say that when their guy comes off the green they don't want to know, from the player's body language, if they're walking away with a birdie or a bogey. That's a good ploy. It means that even if shots have been dropped you force yourself back into a positive position. You play a trick on yourself and act like it's all ok.

I've heard that other coaches tell their charges to simply walk tall between shots. Perhaps it's about power-posing, a sense of authority and self-deception: all useful stuff. But perhaps too it's about finding something other than the minutiae of the game to concern yourself with: easier to think about keeping one's shoulders back and head up straight than about complex swing formula. The in-depth stuff should be left for non-tournament play. When the chips are down you must simply go with the basics and trust yourself.

When hopes are too high or fears too pressing it is impossible to find this higher state. Many major championships are won by the player who performs least poorly in the final round, or so it sometimes seems. With so much at stake it's hard to find that silent space where you can play your best. Nicklaus could do it often, 18 times to be precise. He could handle the pressure and said, without arrogance, that in some ways, for him, the majors were the easiest to win because everyone else found them so hard. His game was complete, but more than that his mind would comply with his mighty will to win.

Getting into that unconscious space where the best

golf can be played is to turn one's back on logic and to embrace intuition. It's almost to defy reason and reality. There's no way he can make another consecutive birdie, the casual watcher might think. But somehow the great golfer would find a way.

No doubt even Jack felt nerves creep up on him. But his concentration took him beyond the reaches of such stuff. Nowhere in his books and interviews do we find any mention of the deadly hush of the tee and the watching crowds. For him it was perhaps perfect peace. For others it can be a terrifying atmosphere, a fog of fear so thick with worries that it seems impossible to draw the club back through it. The Ryder Cup, where golfers suddenly find themselves playing not for personal glory but for their friends and countrymen and more fans than they ever knew they had, seems to be one such frightening place. Many have testified that the first tee in the first game is an unnerving environment in which to make a smooth swing, a place where grown men can suddenly shrink. In response to this a new technique has emerged which seems to stop the hands trembling. First adopted by Europe's Ian Poulter and America's Bubba Watson, but no longer confined to these exuberant showmen, the spectators will roar through a golfer's entire swing. The crowds enjoy it and the golfers respond to it, adding yards and forgetting fear. It's easier, it turns out, to play through that cacophony than the deafening silence they normally endure. Oh well, the old-timers say. It's The Ryder Cup and these things come to pass. The barbarians will cross the Danube and The Rhine. Rome will fall. The Crowns will be united. The Enlightenment Period will end.

A state of unconscious fearlessness is desirable. Whereas its inverse, the state of conscious fear, is no place to be with a golf club to hand. It's the place where even the smallest, simplest shots – especially the smallest, simplest shots – become almost impossible. The fine motor skills switch off and the easiest of things becomes a slog. We can all walk across a floor and up some stairs, but when there's a global audience of millions watching us collect our statuette, then it becomes a trickier proposition.

Golfers talk about the yips. Or rather, they don't talk about the yips lest they prove to be contagious. Many a great golfer, especially in middle age, with many thousands of short putts already safely negotiated, has fallen victim to this disease. Perhaps it's caused by overuse, a short-circuit in the system when performing a task we believe we know very well.

There's nothing good about the yips. Maybe the mystery at the heart of them is interesting. Possibly the name itself, to the non-golfer, has a happy sound, a sort of Scottish cadence, the term apparently having been coined by Tommy Armour from Edinburgh, an early 20th Century winner of the US and UK national open competitions as well as The PGA Championship. Whatever it is, there's no cure. There are restoratives: fat handles, long shafts and altered grips. But less than, say, the shank, the yips are not a swing fault. They're a brain fault, a disruption of the ideal condition where, suddenly, the smooth putting stroke is inflicted with an unstoppable twitch.

They exist in many sports where to think too much about a process is to ruin its fluidity. In baseball, the name synonymous with the disease is that of Steve Blatts, the great Pittsburgh Pirates pitcher who suddenly could not do the most natural thing he had ever known and release the ball at the right moment in his throw. It ended his career. Cricketers have been similarly aggrieved; marksmen can develop an equally ruinous twitch; and 'dartitis' is the name given to the affliction when its sufferer can no longer accurately direct his arrows at the treble 20 or bullseye.

In even worse news for golfers, it's now become widely apparent that yips are not confined to the greens. Tiger Woods introduced us to the sort of golf nobody was familiar with, the greatest, most remarkable shots anyone had ever seen, colossal distances combined with deadly accuracy, and a putter which was always true. Then he went and popularised the driver yips, the two-sided miss we see more and more (something I blame on oversize clubs and longer shafts). And as if that wasn't enough, Tiger only went and brought to our attention the short game yips, the bladed chips and the fat chunked shots which he put on show to unsuspecting audiences during his troubled comebacks.

The yips: a strange scourge on the happy sportsman. Dismiss them. Find your flow. Forget you read this.

Never try. Or at least, try not to try. Attempting to be funny often doesn't work. Pursuing happiness is no way to find it. Trying to hit it a mile means mistiming your swing. Seek results indirectly. Put effort into practise and put effortlessness into your game. But don't try to remember all that when you step onto the tee...

More even than the great parks of London – Blackheath and Wimbledon Common – the linksland at Westward Ho! is the crucible of golf in England. This is Royal North Devon Golf Club and it is often referred to as Westward Ho!, the Victorian seaside town where it can be found and which took its name from the (then very popular) Charles Kingsley novel, exclamation mark and all!

Royal North Devon Golf Club has the oldest course in England. What you get today is not the rough track played here in the 1850s, nor exactly the course Old Tom Morris laid out in 1860. But it is the course Herbert Fowler designed in 1908, almost entirely unchanged. You hear such a thing and you make assumptions: the course must be a quirky, old-fashioned seaside entertainment. You read that the clubhouse is a museum full of ancient clubs, watercolours and gold medals: you assume golf must take second place to the management of insurance policies. Apparently, sheep and horses make their way across this common land: alarm bells ring telling you this is the sort of place for history buffs but not for the wider contemporary golf world.

I've made such assumptions before – about Lahinch and Prestwick - and been far off the mark. And playing Royal North Devon I am confounded again. It's 6,600 yards from the back tees which is more than modern enough for a links where there is infinite variety in the wind and indeed infinite variety on the course. The opening holes play fairly flat alongside deep wide streams heading for the sea; next, a fabulous section enters wonderful dunes and makes the most of them; then the course becomes tough and narrow played amongst reeds which are frighteningly sharp – the bitter weeds of England - able to spear a golf ball at 250 yards (they say), responsible too for the (supposed) profusion of one-eyed dogs which frequent the beaches around here; and finally there's a long finish of two big par-3s, two big par-4s and a proper par-5.

Royal North Devon has produced great golfers in the past, Horace Hutchison and JH Taylor chief amongst them, and it's still producing them in the 21st Century. At the end of my first visit I walk off the course and nod to Jimmy Mullen, the instantly recognisable local hero. The tall blonde boy is practising his short game, headphones on, entirely in the flow until I come along. Jimmy was then an amateur prodigy, readying himself for a Walker Cup where he'd win all his matches. I marveled silently at the number of consistently sub-par rounds this kid produced to achieve a +4 handicap on a challenging links which counts mighty Atlantic winds and colossal distracting waves amongst its defences.

Wandering this course, or walking the beaches here, there's some harmony between us and the universe. The barmen – local sailors – understand the complex tides and sand bars which shape them. The ebb and flow is hypnotic. Over the unique pebble ridge the sun breaks out and briefly Saunton, in the distance, is luminous.

I visit again on the first day of winter golf rates. The course is quiet, the time of year when golfers begin to reduce their commitment to the game, when they take their eye off the ball and find their kids have grown up and their partner has left them. The weather is still fine. I go out late, doubling my financial advantage by playing at the twilight price. I'm the last man on the course, playing fast to finish before sunset.

In no time, it seems, I'm on the back nine. Things come around fast, in golf as in life. Not even the slow moving fourball I catch and play through can entirely stop time. Without doubt, this is the state of flow, the mind like water (as the Zen Masters would have it). The 12th hole is entrancing. I begin to visualise the shot I'm to hit, the shot I'm to hit perfectly. It will be a low raking draw. We visualise shots in golf because Jack Nicklaus told us he did it. But no doubt golfers long before him had been doing something similar.

It's easy to picture what we should do. We don't have to concern ourselves, in our little moment of dreaming, with anything else. So we make our mental picture and the only thing between that dream swing and the perfect strike is ourselves, our all too feeble selves. I hit a high slice.

It's commonplace to visualise the shot we want to play. It really is good advice, helping us tap into the memories of good shots gone before. It often works. But for those of us less useful than Nicklaus it often doesn't and in this way it reminds us of life and the sometimes colossal distance between desiring and doing.

This is old-fashioned golf here on the English coast. Why do I like it so very much? Strategy is required on a course like this, yet unlike many modern courses, the strategy that's required is flexible. Almost all these holes can be played in various ways depending on skill and luck and natural elements. The majority of modern strategic courses demand such and such a strategy. Here – and elsewhere in the world of 19th century golf – things are often a little more ambiguous.

It's a wonderful life, I think. Bartenders pull pints. Vicars save souls. Bankers screw people. But golf writers seek a state of flow and live the dream!

The Northam Burrows, the land where the links is laid out, can be busy: golfers, walkers, animals, cars taking surfers to the beach too. But by late afternoon the hustle has died down. Real life recedes a little, but the things that count – surviving and succeeding – are still part of whatever I'm trying to do on the course. Golf, when fully focussed upon, can be the testing ground for real things.

In the final years of World War II the beach here at Westward Ho! was used in the trials of an experimental weapon, The Panjandrum. Two tall wooden wheels were attached to a central barrel filled with explosives, its purpose to smash through the concrete fortifications of the Atlantic Wall which the Nazis had built along the coasts of occupied Northern European countries. Powered by cordite rockets attached to the wheels, this invention of the Admiralty's Directorate of Miscellaneous Weapons Development was basically a giant firework which, during three unsuccessful tests on the sand here, smashed the silence and careered off course while naval top brass and boffins dived for cover.

The project was abandoned but lives on in comedy films and television shows as well as in a slightly whimsical reconstruction staged by a local book festival. Some say the entire thing was a hoax, an attempt to bamboozle the German high command about the nature, timings and location of the inevitable Allied invasion.

Churchill said that a pessimist sees the difficulty in every opportunity and that an optimist sees the opportunity in every difficulty. Probably The Panjandrum was meant to work. Perhaps its failure was a lesson and some good came of it, the Axis Powers putting much needed energy and resource into defending against it.

My driving has been off today. Actually, it's been off for years. But on the final hole I split the fairway and generate the distance I know is in there, occasionally, somewhere inside. The shot comes off, it seems, like a missile. On the testing ground of the home hole I feel like I show my mind who is really the boss here.

The sea air has a vigour that clears the head. At the same time the coastal conditions are enervating and I'm ready to rest. Why do we love golf? There is a buoyancy in flow, a serenity 'in the zone'. It's challenging, refreshing and, when we wake from the golfing dream, it proves to have been agreeably tiring too. I golf therefore I am inclined to count my blessings.

17 UNDER SAIL, 4360

Promptly, at break of day, the storm clears. Through the night it was all roaring skies and blinding lights. But it's calm now and the BBC's Shipping Forecast, the radio broadcast Britain's maritime community once depended on and which a nation now finds simply dependable, offers some reassurance to this landlubber.

When we tune in we should perhaps think of those in peril on the sea, not golfing conditions around the country. But I can't help it:

Cromarty (all is calm in Dornoch, clearing skies, glorious golfing prospects); Forth (it's blowing a bit from Carnoustie through St Andrews, down to East Lothian where it might be tricky up on Gullane Hill); Humber (the wind's up here too for the golfers at Hunstanton and Brancaster); Malin (wet and windy for my Aunt

Esther if she goes out for 12 at Shiskine and probably worse than that over at Rosapenna and Ballyliffin in Ireland where the waves pound furiously on the beach no matter what the Shipping Forecast says); Irish Sea (those on Pat's personal links will suffer a little today); Fastnet (if Loyal ventures out at Cork he'll have seen heftier weather in his time); Lundy (golf will be played in relative calm at Royal North Devon).

Crucially the news for Biscay, famous for its huge swell, is as good as one might hope for in October. "Westerly 4 or 5 becoming variable 3 or 4. Slight or moderate. Showers, thundery at first in south. Moderate or good."

I hear the call of the running tide and I pack my travel sickness pills.

From home in South Somerset it's a yomp across the fields to the train station then a short ride to Westbury where the enigmatic, unexplained white horse, carved in chalk on a hillside above the town, is a strange sight, ancient and English, foreign and frightening to a Scotsman. From here the Portsmouth train plods south through Salisbury and then west along the Channel coastline. I walk through the port's pedestrianised town centre then along the side of a motorway slip road, soon reaching the international ferry terminal.

It's a less than glamorous way to get here, but the ferry is all glamour to me. I've never been on a cruise ship proper, but this is close. Certainly, it's a far cry from frequent ferry crossings I've made from Holy-head to Dublin working on a book about Ireland's greatest golf holes, hiding in John the photographer's camper van and sleeping there in the groaning garage decks or else, if travelling by car, heading up to the public areas and making a pillow of my golf shoes and sleeping on the benches, woken every five minutes by the sound of pops from ring pulls on beer cans or else the screams and roars of fighting gypsies (really).

The Cap Finistère (end of the earth), sails out of Ports-mouth harbour, past the crumbling remains of a con-temporary navy and the spectacular glory of times past, HMS Victory. We will head round the Isle of Wight, across the Channel and follow the line of the French shore to Northern Spain, landing at Santander in 24 hours' time (not carrying on round the coast to Trafalgar where Victory once signalled to the sailors of its outnumbered fleet that so much was expected of them).

The crossing is smooth. The sun sets into the west-ern ocean. I eat and drink like a King because this is a French ferry service. But in bed I sleep fitfully, the gentle roll of the ship, the glass of wine and the cheese board playing havoc with my REM sleep.

Now and then I wake and open the curtains and look to portside, imagining I might see the French coast. But no, there's just blackness, immense emptiness. Seatime is dreamtime and steadily we sail into a new time zone.

The morning arrives and soon everyone is on deck enjoying late summer Spanish sunshine and dead calm seas, drinking coffee and reading paperbacks, holiday-style in the gloriously enforced absence of that day's newspapers and internet connectivity.

A wonderful Anthony Burgess short story, historical fiction at its most speculative, sees Shakespeare and his fellow actors, The King's Men – amongst them Dick Burbage (the first man to play The Dane) and Robert Armin (the company's finest clown, famously Fest in Twelfth Night) – make this same trip, getting so seasick they almost die. The story begins 'We landed at Santander in filthy weather'. I've read the story often and thus the Bay of Biscay has always worried me. But there's been no need. A great journey, one worth creating for storytelling purposes, no doubt works best with some drama. But this has been without jeopardy, without any queasiness.

We land at Santander in fabulous weather and I make my way to the Los Reginas ferry which will take me across the bay. 20 minutes later I step ashore in the little town of Pedrena. There are many barking dogs and fewer pavements, a couple of old men asleep on plastic chairs outside empty cafes. I walk along the main road which is lined with unfinished domestic building projects. Occasionally someone looks at me like they've never seen someone carrying a set of golf clubs, ever. Yet this little town is home to a classic Harry Colt golf course. It's also the home of Ramon

Sota, an early star of The European Tour and mentor to his four nephews, all professional golfers, all born and bred here: Baldomero, Manuel, Vicente and the baby of the family, Severiano.

I check into the hotel, a lovely little unlit posada, all dark wood and lace. Francisco, the proprietor, speaks no English. I have no Spanish, well, a few words, which adds up to rudeness really, the needs of a baby: food, drink and toilets. But Francisco knows why I'm here and he presents me with a glass of water and a few old golf books.

It will be dark soon but I make for the golf club, just to familiarise myself, just to get a first look before tomorrow's early start. About 200 yards from the posada I almost jump out of my skin at the roar of a giant German Shepherd. From a little house behind the red-roofed church of San Pedro where Severiano's funeral took place, this beast terrorises whoever walks past. Turns out though I'm the only person who ever walks past. In the next 36 hours, making eight passes, steeling myself each time, I will never fail to be terrified when it throws itself hard at the high but flimsy fence. I just don't have the cajunas not to flinch. It's the biggest German shepherd I've ever seen and it doesn't bark. It roars like a T Rex (probably). Only on my final pass, two cervezas, a Real Golf Club de Pedrena Club Sandwich and my best round of the year under my belt, do I not move a muscle but laugh in the face of canine terror.

The course and the club itself are fabulous, all Bermuda grasses, beautiful rich families and crocodile logos on cashmere cardigans. Europeans have made golf into what it perhaps should be: a fashion show of continental chic and idle richness. I walk a couple of holes before heading out for food to a little café, El Culebrero. It once boasted the town's first television where the young Severiano used to watch boxing matches, his face pressed on the windows outside. This is how it would be for him: always a fighter, often an outsider. After winning The Masters in 1980 he spoke with his hero, Muhammed Ali. During their conversation the heavyweight called the golfer 'the greatest'. Seve's tape recording of the conversation would always be amongst his most prized belongings. (The greats require affirmation too. Seve liked hearing it from Ali. But perhaps Ali was one of the few who didn't require outside testimony to his worth.)

First thing next morning I'm back at Real Golf de Pedrena, playing the eccentric little nine-holer which the town's most famous son designed. It's utterly beguiling and many would complain about its odd lengths and angles. But I like it so much I play it again before the day really heats up. Then, back at the posada, Francisco serves me many weighty Cantabrian breads, sticky cakes and endless sweet coffee for my late late breakfast, enough to sink a ship. I had no idea the Spanish ate such big breakfasts. And I have absolutely no idea how they manage to get back to sleep just a couple of hours from now following such a heavy feast. But mid-morning I'm ready for the real thing, the championship course, the 1928 Harry Colt layout where Seve unlocked his genius.

The first plays away from the clubhouse, the ideal short par-4. The second, a long par-3, plays towards the boundary wall. I'm looking at almost 200 yards into a gentle maritime wind. My 3-iron falls just above the flag and rolls to maybe 12 feet. I take two putts. I look up. Here is the wall Seve climbed as a child to sneak onto the course he couldn't afford to play, hopping over it for a few stolen holes. Another 200 yards away is the house he bought as a successful adult. From there – always childlike – he would hit long irons from the garden down onto this very green.

It's a charming course and inspiration is never far away. It's easy, here, today, to play well. Under the late summer sun, making my way through Pedrena's early fallen leaves and pine straw, the game is ideal. To golf well you have to be, partially, free from desire. Freedom from desire is wonderful, energising. There's no pride and therefore no sorrow. Seve probably always had too much desire, too much pride and subsequently, we feel, some sorrow.

The course is up and down and side to side. In places just the walking requires fuerza (strength: my fifth Spanish word). No wonder Seve had back problems. But the whole thing feels like a sound convergence between the manmade and the natural, never bombastic. The course is spread out over a heavily wooded hillside, a peninsula really with water on three sides. Views over the estuary to Santander are romantic and glorious.

Maybe if my game was off it would be less enjoyable, but maybe not. It can be pretty tough when you're not playing well. But as a sport, as a game, there's no loss no matter how poorly you play. Something can always be gained or learned. And of course, golfers are fortunate to play a game where if they don't succeed they can try and try again, because you never know what can happen. Seve, I suppose, couldn't adopt this view, not in public anyway. Early on he needed success to overcome his humble beginnings, a bit like the prize fighters he so admired. Later on he needed success because we expected it of him; he did too.

Yet, I wonder, does golf make us happy the better we get? Look at late 19th century Young Tom Morris. Look at late 20th century David Duval.

Today, however, my sound form is adding some small joy to the day. The end of the round is approaching all too soon. I wasn't going to look at my scorecard and perform any calculations. You're not meant to. And the 17th is a difficult drive with a narrow fairway, or the illusion of one. I know I should play away, enjoy myself, put no pressure on myself. But I also know that to not take golf seriously, to not feel a little heat, is not to extract the maximum pleasure. I look at the card. I know what I need and somehow get it.

I don't want to overstate the case. This little pilgrimage is of no greater consequence. How could it be when it's been so self-indulgent? But here on the golf course I've been focussed, alert, escaping the rudderless drift of my nature. And I imagine I've earned some kinship with golf's great matador. It's easy today. Seve, often, in the early days, found golf to be easy.

Thinking back to when I learned to play, I imagine the game was harder. In fact, I'm convinced of it. The small wooden wood, the wee wound golf ball: it was difficult but pleasing. The sound of my battered John Letters persimmon driver on a reclaimed balata ball was more beautiful than the composite clank of my current large headed Callaway. Of course, I didn't know the game was harder then. I now occasionally practise with an old 4-wood and I'm satisfied that it helps my ball-striking because it's a tougher task. But the days of persimmon woods are gone forever. I miss their somehow precious, certainly beautiful, gorgeous grain, the perfect patina seen beneath a smooth gloss.

I'm suspecting, because choices must be made and economics must be applied, that I'll never return here to Pedrena. It's not that it's anything less than wonderful, but life is short and there's only so much that can be done, only so many things which should be revisited. But the 18th hole, the 3-iron then the 9-iron both straight out of the middle of the middle, get me thinking I have to return. That's golf. The perfect hit will call you back through the ages. The closing hole here is not remarkable, though it has lovely elevation. And I feel I'll be replaying it for years to come, in my mind.

It's with regret that I leave Seve's old golf club. But 36 holes in a single day feels like a proper return on this quick trip.

The shadow of the night comes on and I walk across the road bridge to the neighbouring town of Soma. Car headlights are being switched on and I'm intermittently dazzled. But I'm walking above the beach where Seve learned the game and it's a thrill.

Dave Cannon, the photographer, told me about a magazine photoshoot he did here with Seve, his hero, the subject of some of his greatest photos, and ultimately – with a tear in his eye – his friend. Dave had flown in from Australia, connected to Bilbao and drove to Seve's home. He was tired and Northern Spain was cold. They made their way down to this beach to recreate Seve learning to play golf as a child. He reckons it's the best two hours he's ever had taking photos.

Seve found an old tin can in a hedge, picked up a stick and took a handkerchief from his pocket. These he made into a golf hole. He started putting to it, with a long-iron as he used to. Then he moved into longer shots, eventually full swing sequences off the rock-hard sand, clean and perfect, rifled into the distance. When all the balls had been hit and many photographs taken, Dave, jetlagged and chilly, got his camera gear together and began to move back to Seve's

Craig Morrison

Range Rover. "No, no, Dave," said his subject. "Now we collect the balls."

I'm not sure how well this reflects on Dave's environmental commitments, both the long-haul flights and abandoning the golf balls. Still, it reflects well on Seve. He started with nothing and valued what he had.

In Somo I eat in a little local place called Restaurant Melly. It's functional yet phenomenal: baclau, spinach and chickpeas; then meatballs with tomato and bread sauce; a carafe of red wine; lemon mousse; then coffee; and with the moderate bill, just 12 euros, comes a ridiculously large glass of the local spirit Orujo de Potes. Dining alone is entirely cheerful when the food's good and the price is right and life is interesting and when you have some decent books. Inevitably, the books I have are about the great man.

He used to hit the ball a mile, insane distances, winning long drive competitions against the lengthiest. His immodest range of shots – from dynamite drives to perfect putts – were something to behold. But somehow he came unstuck. And so Seve's golfing greatness is somehow forgotten, perhaps because he played for a long time as a truly poor golfer: short, inaccurate and disappointed.

Seve won five Majors, pretty much the accepted yardstick for greatness. He won three Opens and two Masters and it could have been more, not US Opens or PGAs but more Opens and Masters. He collided with fate at Augusta in 1986 when Nicklaus reached the magic number. But mostly, like most golfers, he collided with himself. In this respect he was the everyman, which is why he was well loved by the public. In other respects he was an incomparable genius, which is also why he was so adored. (Another thing about winning the big events: for him, all those Majors were played away from home. It's easiest to bring home Major titles if you're American and next easiest if you're British.) Including all tournaments he won 87. His reputation is, rightly, greater than his statistics. Yet it's no mean haul, astonishing really.

He won a million dollars in the US and in Europe in one season when such a thing was unheard of. He was the first European to win The Masters, paving the way for Langer, Lyle, Woosnam, Faldo, Olazabal and others, His Ryder Cup record is phenomenal. Tony Jacklin, Europe's greatest Ryder Cup Captain, cites his favourite cup memory not as some glorious champagne spraying moment in front of adoring crowds but as the time he first set out to try to build a European team and Seve, pushed out by the establishment and his own pig-headedness, agreed to come back into the fold. "Tony, I will do my very best to help you," he said. Seve's influence in Europe is endless. And his style is unforgettable, his attitude too, for better and worse. Seve was a golfer who would sometimes access the 'deeper magic'. When he could he was unstoppable. But he couldn't always find it. And despite the Dickensian backstory, the humble beginnings and great achievements, his life was no fairytale.

Where did it all go wrong (as the room service guy said to George Best entering his hotel room to deliver a bottle of champagne and finding him in bed with Miss World)? Well, it's not that it went horribly wrong. It's more that life is rarely entirely simple and, well, things happen. He first hurt his back when he was 14, boxing inevitably. Then three years later, playing the Spanish under 25s at Pedrena, his back really began to hurt, probably because he'd practised so hard for this tournament so determined was he to win it; and he did win it, achieving his first victory as a professional on his home course in his home town, something many would love to do.

But let's say it wasn't his back. Let's say it was something else. We might skip forward to his 4-iron on the 15th hole in the final round of The Masters in '86. The sound of the ball hitting the water was probably louder to him down the years than the sound of the roaring crowd as the old stager, Nicklaus, ploughed his way through the field. Self-certainty is vital to good golf. After that tournament, where Seve realised his destiny might sometimes be second to someone else's, the confidence waned. Then the following year he missed a short putt on the 10th in the playoff and, really, he was never the same again.

He began the tinkering that Nick Faldo had popularised. The Englishman had got a swing coach and a new swing and it was like Coco Chanel getting a tan: suddenly everyone wanted one. Sandy Lyle became a tinkerer too and he got worse for it. Same with Seve, although in both those cases they only began delving into the mechanics when things were already going wrong by which time it was possibly too late. Faldo's genius had been to bravely make the change while swinging smoothly.

Getting involved with the swing didn't work for Seve. So, he started looking into the mind. He and his one-time coach and confidant Mac O'Grady went into the desert and ceremonially buried his swing, digging a hole in the sand and dumping his old clubs and photos and videos in it. If true, they were mad as hatters...

Seve's brother, Baldomero, reckoned that between the ages of 14 and 18 was when Seve played his greatest golf, never missing a shot. Back then, little Seve had nothing. I could be dreaming – just because I'm travelling light on a small budget and I've been golfing well – but when we own too much we fear too much because we have things to lose. I have no real attachment to this place; I'm carrying little, just a half set and my slightly utilitarian laptop; I undoubtedly cut an odd figure around here; but I feel strangely free. With fewer possessions we rediscover a little of our humanity, our natural state. It was Seve's natural state to be an amazing, instinctive golfer. There's a fearless purity to having no attachments. Cares soon show themselves on the golfer.

The rampant consumerism of recent times makes me think spiritual communities will enjoy something of a renaissance. Golf has some of the elements required to be part of this. It's had everything necessary for the materialist times and it has what's needed for gentler times. That's partially the theme, depending on how you read it, of the best-selling golf novel of all time, *Golf in the Kingdom*. It's something pro golfers suffering a dip in form could learn from or at least try. Cast off your belongings! Stop wearing the sponsored cap. Fly cattle class. Give your winnings to charity. You'll be happy, meaningful, well-loved and you'll shoot low (maybe).

The young Severiano had little. No doubt the things he achieved and the things he owned attached themselves to him. I imagine he wanted some of his youthful freedom back.

What was good came from within, his natural brilliance. Anything from without – including swing advice from tried and tested professionals – he railed against and so he found himself dispirited and occasionally – it appeared to some - darkly depressed.

On my final morning I walk along the coast path to the town's little nine-holer, Junquera. It's a once-in-a-lifetime course (never again) but there's fun to be had on it. I pay a nominal sum at the ticket shed and play off the astroturf-covered first tee with a couple of old boys who join me. We can't communicate, apart from a few congratulations and condolences delivered in the international language of golf. They're not talking to each other much either, though I can tell that they're ancient friends.

The Cantabrian people are nothing like the southern Mediterranean Spanish. Meeting them, I'm amazed that Seve was so flamboyant. These people have much in common, apparently, with Celts, though nobody's sure what a Celt is. Anyway, these guys have some Celtic reticence about them, perhaps still remembering their Trojan ancestors fleeing Greeks or their post-Roman Iron Age uncles struggling to adapt. Whatever, we're happy in one another's company.

When I was a kid I could feel fairly grown up playing golf: winning and losing, giving putts or asking them to be holed, trying to be brave on a busy first tee. But as a man it often makes me feel like a kid again, just getting away from it all, just doing my thing. I feel like that on the course in Junquera with the Cantabrians, saying little, just going about our golf as best we can. Nobody's playing perfectly. But we're right in the middle of the sweet spot found in leisure, the place where what is meaningful and what is meaningless converge pleasantly. All journeys reveal a destination the traveller wasn't necessarily aiming for. I had no plans to play any golf here, not with Seve's home club less than a mile away. But this has been especially enjoyable.

Back at the posada I pick up my things, settle the bill and say adios to Francisco. The little boat takes me back to Santander. The young Severiano made this trip often. Even as a rich and famous man the simple geography of the natural harbour would have made it practical.

Inevitably – like all romantic Scotsmen on the waves – I'm thinking of The Skye Boat Song, not the popular cloying words I knew when I was a child, but the Robert Louis Stevenson lyric I learned later:

Give me again all that was there
Give me the sun that shone
Give me the eyes, give me the soul
Give me the lad that's gone.

I spend a couple of hours in Santander, enjoying its lovely older buildings, marvelling at how Iberian business works when its shops – all strictly specialist – are shut for so many hours in the middle of the day. If I wanted lingerie, handbags, shoes or jamon this would be the place to come. But I'd have to pick my moment. I do though find a stall which sells me an ice cream before boarding the ship.

The return sailing is less enjoyable than the outward leg, inevitably. The weather's spectacular but the ship is rolling. The Bay of Biscay in those first few hours is distinctly choppy. I don't eat. I don't drink. I sit in my cabin feeling sick, worrying about next month's rent and doing some writing. (It's not as fulfilling as it sounds.)

Pulling away from the dock, the back of the boat,

the helicopter deck with a sweeping view to the rear and to both sides, is full of elderly sun-worshipers, large and fairly immodest. They take part in a feeding frenzy for plastic deckchairs which the crew produce. Then they peel off and hitch up their garments.

So, I can't take in the panoramic view from the stern and have to make a choice between portside, to say farewell to Santander, or starboard, for Pedrena.

I say goodbye to Pedrena.

18 SOLOGNE, 3610

E arly golf, we know, was played in the Low Countries, then established in Scotland. Before that though, before it made its way to Flanders and The Netherlands, golf-like club and ball games were played in France.

Illustrations from a 15th Century prayer book belonging to the Duchess of Burgundy show such amusements. One of them is very golf-like, probably Paillemaille. The argument goes that this was the precursor to the game we know, that this game made its way to Flemish parts, no doubt elsewhere too (think Pall Mall in London), and eventually to Scotland.

But Scots complain. Forget these foreign imports and historical mutations. From our land came the game. Its first ever mention was in a 1457 edict from King James II of Scotland who banned 'ye golf' along with football. This is compelling stuff for Scotsmen. But those who favour the continental beginnings, be they Dutch or earlier still French, say 'ye golf' was probably a disruptive team game, some sort of marauding version of the Royal & Ancient pastime, a bit like The Ryder Cup!

No matter: that Burgundy may have begat golf appeals to me. As a teenager I'd golfed there with my French penpal, Arnaud, at a course owned by Formula 1 legends, Alain Prost and Jacques Lafitte. There was another part-owner too, a businessman whose business was motorsport safety and whose daughter was Arnaud's girlfriend. We were his guests. I vividly remember Arnaud putting his foot down hard on the accelerator of the golf cart. But it was in reverse... We ran pretty much right over his girlfriend's little brother, our host's son. I don't remember the sound of the reversing alarm. Maybe they didn't exist back then. It was a terrible moment. Amazingly there were only cuts and bruises. And as the innocent and unhurt party, I now remember it with some fondness and occasional late-onset post-trauma hilarity.

Anyway, it turns out there's no need to return to Burgundy (where, in any case, Arnaud and I are banned from all courses). The illustrations in the Burgundy manuscript actually show the games being played in the Loire Valley with its distinctive Chateaux in the background.

They still play golf in The Loire. And by happy coincidence one of the world's truly great courses can be found there: Les Bordes.

Baron Bich saw the future. He didn't know the specifics: that reversing alarms would become so loud and ubiquitous; that social media would be sometimes so antisocial; that we'd be so connected to computer screens we would never switch off and develop musculoskeletal disorders from overuse. But he saw enough to believe that the most prized future commodity would be silence.

With that in mind the French industrialist bought a huge estate in rural France and built a golf course there, Les Bordes. His fortune was amassed through a high-volume / low-cost business model, but was spent on low-volume / high-cost pursuits, specifically sailing and high-end golf. His products were famously disposable and mass-produced, his passions far less so.

Bic razors and Bic lighters sold, and still sell, in massive quantities globally. But his masterstroke – apart from dropping the H from the end of his name for branding purposes – was to buy a patent for a pen from a Hungarian inventor named Biro.

In the 50s and 60s, from The Baron's factories in Paris and around the world, 10s of millions of these pens were produced daily. Each could draw a straight line for more than two miles before running out. They are simple and perfect. They still sell strongly today.

The hexagonal barrel, like a typical pencil, gives optimal grip. Its flat sides prevent it rolling off uneven tables. That they are (mostly) transparent means you know when they need to be replaced. To ease ink flow a small hole in the barrel's body keeps the air pressure equal inside and outside the pen. An extra hole in both cap and tube will stop those who chew their pens from choking on them. And the Bic Cristal, to use its proper name, is the ideal implement to perform an emergency tracheotomy...

We learn to appreciate simpler things as we get older. Perhaps children enjoy the retractable multi-colour Bic pens. But grown-ups probably take more pleasure from signing important documents with the black or blue Bic, the clear barrel for the medium point or maybe the orange barrel for the finer point.

Whatever, it's a work of genius. And, truthfully, not just for the sake of synchronicity, Les Bordes is too.

At Beaugency one heads south over the glorious 26 span bridge across The Loire, where Joan of Arc defeated the English in the 15th century and where 500 years later Nazi troops surrendered to French Resistance forces. We are entering The Sologne, a region of pools and lakes amongst the deep dark sandy forests between The Loire and The Cher, the setting for Alain Fournier's intense and strange little novel, *Le Grand Meaulnes*. Somewhere here its hero stumbles on a magical estate and his life – and that of his friends – is changed forever. Whatever he found can never be rediscovered. He will forever search for something unobtainable.

In English translation its problematic title has been given as *The Lost Domain*, *The Wanderer* and *The End of Youth*. You get the idea: it's an enigmatic book. In France its reputation is similar to that of *The Catcher in the Rye* in America. And it has something of that book's brilliant immaturity and improbability, though none of its humour.

This is deep France, la France profonde. Down dense forest tracks one eventually finds what one seeks.

"An extraordinary feeling of contentment raised his spirits, a feeling of perfect, almost intoxicating tranquillity: the certainty that he had reached his goal and that henceforth only happiness awaited him."

It's an Indian summer evening on the continent. We sit outside on leather sofas. It's that kind of place (and I mean it in a good way). We feel the chill and go in for supper. The log fires are burning. This is hunting lodge, turned clubhouse, turned fabulous restaurant. A big-time US television producer is visiting. He's golf mad. His wife's golf mad. His little kid's golf mad. We're talking about his friend, Larry David, who's famously mad. When this TV producer first introduced Larry to his wife someone present said, "isn't she lovely Larry?" Larry said nothing. The question was asked again. "Right," Larry said. "But isn't she beautiful?" he was asked again. "What do you want me to say?" he demanded. "Say she's beautiful," continued the person who didn't know when to quit. "Ok," says Larry. But he didn't say it.

It's the producer's wife telling us this. She's laughing and, of course, she's beautiful. (So much hearsay and idle gossip for a golf book, I know, but Larry's a golfer. I've read that he sits in the back seat of his limo with the clubs because he won't put them in the trunk. And he plays golf with presidents too. He might be a crazy golfer, but he's one of us.)

We talk historical drama. The producer's had some serious successes with the genre. We have differences of opinion, not least my talking about costume drama and him about tunic dramas. He says the British versions do the talk but not the walk. "You've got to do the walk and the talk." I'll obsess over this for years to come and I think he's right.

But all this is just preamble. Next morning I'm on the practise ground (so still the preamble) but it's getting exciting now. What a practise ground it is! My divots are swept away speedily. We are getting everything ready. We're not there yet, but this is an important part of the whole ceremony. (Despite coming from the land practise ground's forgot, I love a good range session...)

I'm playing with Mark Vickery, the Director of Golf, who does the walk and the talk. He'd perhaps be out-gunned on tour these days but his golf's glorious, his putting a joy forever. His John Letters Silver Goose putter is an ancient thing of beauty and he wields it like the true bearer of the Subtle Knife...

He tells me about 'la danse du golf.' A previous incumbent of his post developed a teaching method under this name. It's relaxed and easy, a natural turn back and forth. It's not exactly careless. It's not meant to be reckless. But it is deliberately loose. I'm finding it helpful. People say you should dance like nobody's watching. Sure enough, I do my best dancing alone in front of the mirror, my best singing alone in the shower and, often, my best golf alone on the range. And I'm inclined right now to believe that the golf swing is a dance, which probably explains much about my own game.

Mark was brought up by his grandparents in an English coalmining family and as a teenager turned pro at his local club. When he landed a job at the prestigious Sunningdale Golf Club the world suddenly opened up to him.

His instruction – which I ask for - comes first with compliments. "It's lovely the way you do this. Now do this too" and he offers up something simple which makes the next two days go with a swing.

I drag from him self-deprecating stories about golf with Woosie and Seve, great days on a fledgling European Tour. He doesn't boast or brag. And I think about how, writing and promoting a book, I'm going to have to boast and brag in order to sell it. This is the new way. We must all compete for attention. But I like a golfer who doesn't boast, who lets his 'clubs do the talking'. Mark's ancient John Letters Silver Swan putter speaks for him. Honestly, the guy never misses.

The course is precise, silent, focussed inside the wild nature which surrounds it. There's a concentrated purity to it. Oh, and it's beautiful and it's hard. And the greens are soft and receptive, as well as entirely true and ferociously fast. Any golfer will be inspired. I'm inspired. But fear creeps in. There's a lot of water. The fairways don't roll. So the golfer needs long carries and accuracy. Yet for nuance Les Bordes cannot be beaten.

Lunch is like the course, long and lovely. We drink chilled red Saumur. It looks like maybe I did something right, once, in a previous life (maybe before I was married).

In the afternoon we play again. Mark tells me to swing out more. I am playing with too much fear. Golf is about confidence and sometimes exuberance, capturing some youthful arrogance and belief. To be in control you have to be out of control. This is not especially Mark's way of playing. But it's so far removed from mine that I have to be pushed in this direction just to find a sensible middle-ground.

For the back nine I'm on my own. But I've got Mark's traditional, quite old fashioned, weighted practise club with me. It's the sort of thing you see advertised on obscure golf channels in the middle of the night. But it works for me. The weight clicks over a latch which you set according to the swing speed you're aiming for. You're trying to achieve this at the bottom of the swing, where you hit the ball, maybe just beyond that point to guarantee acceleration. Soon – and it's often the way, golfing alone – I'm playing free and easy, hitting it further than I have since I was a teenager.

Great golf architecture basically makes one think before striking out and Les Bordes, for sure, represents great architecture. So now I'm thinking that the way to defeat the design is perhaps not to think, not to think too much, to engage in the decision making and then to disengage for the act itself. In golf – in all things – there is a thrill in changing from defensive to offensive, in moving from passive sufferer to aggressive attacker. When the golfer realises he's playing too much in fear, making mistakes because of it, when he changes gear and takes some chances and plays bravely and finds his game improved because of it, well, that's often one of the best sensations the game offers. It's a form of standing up and being counted (on my own, with nobody watching).

The wilds here are truly wild, almost encroaching on the manicured perfections of the course. The juxtaposition is remarkable. The boars and stags must be close too. You might feel vulnerable in the middle of it all.

On one hole a beautiful stone cross stands on the edge of a waste bunker. It's dated 1864, a monument to an earlier owner's teenage son who fell from his horse and died at this spot when stag hunting. It could be a French churchyard. It could be Domaine Romanee Conti. But it's a golf course. And yet it doesn't feel out of place.

There are three other groups on the course this afternoon, 12 guys playing some serious golf. They're led by a businessman from the north of England who used to visit often with his son whose ashes are now scattered in the forest here.

It's late afternoon and a warm wind picks up. The Poplar Tremblants shimmer amongst the silver birches.

Can a golf course be a spiritual place? Rarely. Where profit comes before people it's hard to feel spiritual. It's easier to make a connection where business is not the game. So obscure nine-holers with honesty box systems might be better suited to such things. But Les Bordes, maybe because it's between times – the Baron's reign being over, the commercial potentials now being sized up – affords some spirituality. It's a very special place. So of course it's good for the soul. I pray that it won't become a conurbation course. But in a spirit of generosity I also ask the golfing gods (always plural those sporting pagan deities) that more people get to experience this place. And that is indeed the plan: limited housing and the conversion of the estate's wonderful Chateau de Bel Air into a small hotel.

No doubt much of the genius of the place is, inevitably, down to finance. The flawless conditioning costs much. Impossibly perfect greens don't come cheap. And there's almost nobody here so you can play as fast – or I suppose as slow – as you want. All clubs must crave some of what Les Bordes has: the peace and pace of play chief amongst them. But how to afford such luxuries, they will wonder.

Early evening I'm on the practise ground again, swinging harder, faster, hitting some fabulous shots, then, inevitably, rifling some shots wildly off-line and I'm reminded that golf is also partially about practising restraint. In that respect it's very boring. And also in that respect it's quietly enthralling.

Good technique and the right principles bring about excellent play. But exaggerate those techniques and principles and it can go wrong very quickly.

Dinner is a communal affair of fine food and fine wine, the Hollywood set, the proprietor, the golf pro, the hanger on. Yannick, a red-haired Breton who understands service and gastronomy as only a Frenchman can, produces some '47 Vouvray, the greatest of all Vouvray vintages, more celebrated even than the wine of liberation two years earlier. We eat the pudding. We drink the wine. We share the autumn sunshine of almost 70 years ago and I'm ready to weep. (So, ok, we had a few drinks across the evening.)

At breakfast we eat delicacies delivered by the Beautiful Boulanger of Beaugnecy who causes a stir daily at 6am when she does her rounds. I was up and about early, not to catch a glimpse of the beautiful baker, though I'm happy to have done so, but just to take a walk, take it all in, so that in future I can properly long for this place, a domain lost to me.

An early morning saunter is a great thing. Thoreau, an advocate of a minimum four hours each day wandering fields and woods (which is not to say he'd approve of five and six hour rounds or even golf itself) believed it was an art in itself. The word derives, he reckoned, from wanderers in the Middle Ages seeking charity for their pilgrimage to The Holy Land, the Sainte Terre.

On my final morning I have a couple of hours to spare. I'm on borrowed time. (We're all on borrowed time.) Nine holes can be squeezed in. After a few holes I'm joined by the owner's son and we're just playing, just hitting the ball. I'm hitting it really well because of Mark's advice. The kid's hitting it really well because of Mark's advice. What's so good about hitting the ball? Nothing. But you know how it is. Children, especially, know how it is. Hit a ball and it feels good. Hit a tennis ball with a racket and it's good. Fizz a fast serve into the corner of the box, bouncing past your opponent and it feels better still. Just hit the thing. It's great. Hit the golf ball high enough and you're flying with it. Hit it interestingly enough - with a little fade or draw or backspin - and you're a wizard casting spells.

The kid's dad shows up. He's that unusual thing: a wealthy man who is exceptionally laid back and doesn't play golf. He's here for the peace and quiet, a little business no doubt, but really just to fish for the carp and monstrous pike which we see lurking in the deep ponds.

Golf courses can be profound, I think, either in their orderliness or in their wildness, the way they have tamed nature or given themselves to her. Les Bordes is profound in both ways, like the great gardens, where human culture meets wild nature.

It's three hours down the autoroutes, through the Loire Valley, back to the Atlantic coast, happily listening to some obscure French disco music, eventually reaching La Rochelle. The airport here is only one by dint of its planes, not by its scale or horror. It's tiny. It's painted white. There are palm trees and tents in the courtyard outside, temporary summer structures to shelter the seasonal crowds from the sun. People are dressed in linen. But the seasons are beginning to change. It's la rentrée. Families are now heading home and work beckons.

Delusional as ever, I imagine myself here in a slightly crumpled jacket, reading a day old Scottish newspaper, parlaying the Franglais with local people, looking down my nose at the summer incomers. Maybe I'll keep a small yacht on the island, Île-de-Ré. Of course, when I make this happen there will be no newspapers (luxury items from the past). There will be no linen jackets (space suits being compulsory). There will be no yachts (the oceans having run dry thanks to the byproducts of cheap air travel). And poor, great, glorious golf will be a curiosity from the past, remembered in ancient land forms like stone circles and burial chambers seen only from the air, something future archaeologists will look at and wonder if it was a devotional right humans took part in as they made their journeys into oblivion.

Taking off we look down and see La Rochelle, its mighty harbour and the crumbling U-boat pens.

Just offshore I see Île-de-Ré, the salt flats on the west of the island, beyond them the lighthouse. I can also see the little golf course. It's one of the relatively 'un-written places' in the game. Remote. Removed. Less than brilliant so under the radar.

I played there one morning with my great friend Tony. We were on a joint family holiday. Our first sons were just more than a year old and we cycled off, 15 miles from Le Bois Plage for a quick game.

Tony won, I remember. It was a great morning. We cycled back and had lunch in La Couarade, oysters and inexpensive salty local white wine. Our wives and kids came and met us for ice cream and a stroll in the square.

From the sky I can see it quite clearly. It makes some kind of distant sense. I pick out the curving fifth hole on the edge of the course, hard by the shore, where we could hear the yacht masts in the wind. It felt like Brancaster England or Naples Florida, but better than that we were on our own Atlantic island playing an altogether inconsequential nine-holer.

We're too high up now to pick out individuals. But there'll be a small figure down there on the course somewhere, a few people perhaps playing the closing holes as the sun sinks.

Amongst the dunes, a little bag slung over their shoulders, someone is perhaps seeking a small ball in the wiry grasses. From this height, from any height, they're unimportant, the game they're playing no doubt pointless, a diversion merely. They could - and probably should - be doing something else. But they're busy for now, maybe even giving some little meaning to a moment in their life. Cumulatively, these moments can mean much, distracted from reality, focussed on something else, something which they feel has meaning, which others perhaps do not. In those seconds it probably makes sense to them.

I'm thinking about this and about the book I'm going to write when I get home.

I'm thinking that if this is the answer it must have been a strange question.